W9-DBW-376

WITHDRAWN

CARL A. RUDISILL LIBRARY
LENOIR-RHYNE COLLEGE

GAYLORD

The Management of Personnel

OTHER PUBLICATIONS BY THE AUTHOR

Compensation. New York: AMACOM, 1981.

A Business Approach to Management Development. Vero Beach, Florida: R.B. Keck & Company, Inc., 1978.

Increasing Employee Productivity. New York: AMACOM, 1976.

Managing Professional Services Enterprises. Pitman Publishing Corp., 1971.

Wages and Salaries. New York: AMACOM, 1960.

A Survey of Pension Planning. Chicago: Commerce Clearing House, Inc., 1953.

THE MANAGEMENT OF PERSONNEL

Robert E. Sibson

CARL A. RUDISILL LIBRARY
LENOIR-RHYNE COLLEGE

An R. B. Keck Book
Published by Arrangement with
VANTAGE PRESS
New York / Washington / Atlanta
Los Angeles / Chicago

For Jay

HF
5549
.S5 853
1985
aug. 1996

FIRST EDITION

All rights reserved, including the right of
reproduction in whole or in part in any form.

Copyright © 1985 by Robert E. Sibson

An R. B. Keck Book

Published by arrangement with Vantage Press, Inc.
516 West 34th Street, New York, New York 10001

Manufactured in the United States of America
ISBN: 0-533-06441-4

Library of Congress Catalog Card No.: 84-91344

TABLE OF CONTENTS

Preface vii

1. MANAGEMENT AND PERSONNEL: Our Human Resources; Management of the Work Force; Are Employees Doing Their Best?; A Need for Improved Effectiveness in the Management of Personnel; Evolution of More Effective Methods of Managing Personnel; The Effectiveness of Work; Increasing the Effectiveness of Work 1
2. THE DELEGATIVE METHOD OF MANAGING PERSONNEL: The Programmatic Method of Managing Personnel; The Delegative Method: Policy Management; Guideline Management; Delegative Practices; Quality Management 18
3. THE MANAGERS OF PERSONNEL: The Tradition of Management; The Managers; The Managers of Personnel; Implementation; It Must Be Done 37
4. EMPLOYEE PARTNERS: The Partnership Philosophy; The Environment We Have Created; Management Actions; Specific Practices; Precedents and Cases; Idealism or a Practical Business Objective? 49
5. THE PERSONNEL DEPARTMENT: The Evolution of the Personnel Organization; Basic Organization of the Personnel Department; Increasing the Effectiveness of the Personnel Department; Leadership Companies; Do Better 66
6. BACK TO THE BASICS: Labor Relations; Employment; Information; Managing Compensation Costs; One-Day-at-a-Time Management; Responsibility for the Basics 85
7. LABOR RELATIONS 93
8. STAFFING: Put Your Personnel Dollars Up-Front; Staffing Tools; Vertical Staffing; Future Needs; Manpower Management 101
9. PERSONNEL INFORMATION: The Need for Personnel Information; Human Resources Information Systems; An Informa-

tion System; Data Elements; Interbusiness Comparisons; How to Proceed 110
10. COMPENSATION: Managing Compensation Costs; Competitive Pay; Pricing Jobs; The Sibson Job Evaluation Method; Free Choice; Performance Reward Systems in Business; Some Key Pay Issues 123
11. BENEFIT COST CONTAINMENT: Health Insurance; Retirement Benefits; "Everybenefit"; Special Benefits for Executives 140
12. ORGANIZATIONAL STRUCTURING 149
13. EMPLOYEE COMMUNICATIONS: Basic Flaws in Employee Communications; Company-Initiated Communications; The Company Transponder; Managers as Communicators; Changing Employee Attitudes; Monitoring Communications . 163
14. PERFORMANCE APPRAISAL: Basic Issues; Performance Ratings; Potential Ratings; Evaluative Appraisal of Performance; Evaluative Appraisal of Potential; The Appraisal System 174
15. TRAINING AND DEVELOPMENT: Training-Development; Nonprogrammatic Training; Programmatic Training; Development Processes; Professional Development; More Thoughts on Management Development; Executive Training 187
16. PRODUCTIVITY IMPROVEMENT: Management Overview; Basic Activities Required to Increase Productivity; Measuring Productivity; Methods of Increasing Employee Productivity; The Manager's Job; The Producers; Some Lessons Learned in Productivity Improvement 202
17. PERSONNEL PLANNING: What Is Personnel Planning?; The Importance of Strategic Personnel Planning; Some Guidelines for Effective Strategic Personnel Planning; Personnel Planning Items Should Be Evaluated; Items of Strategic Personnel Planning 218
18. PERSONAL VALUES IN PERSONNEL WORK: Personal Values and Productivity; The Need for Personal Values; Do Personal Values Contribute to Higher Productivity?; Personal Values 228

About the Author 241

PREFACE

This is our book on personnel. It doesn't cover everything in the field or everything of importance. This book contains what we think are the most important matters in personnel today.

There are four parts to this book. The first five chapters cover basic thinking about personnel. The role of personnel and the critical importance of the effective management of personnel keynote the work. A basic style of managing personnel is outlined and recommended. As part of that style of managing, companies must consider again the issue of who the managers are, and my thoughts on that critical matter are covered. I also urge strongly the adoption of a different company attitude toward those who work in the firm, an "employee-partner" philosophy. Finally, in this first part of the book, I make comments and recommendations about the effective management of the personnel department.

The next eleven chapters deal with key personnel practices. Included are my recommendations for managing the basic areas of personnel: staffing, personnel information, labor relations, and management of compensation costs. New organizational structuring guidelines are presented. Fundamentally different and more effective practices in communications, training and development, and performance appraisal are presented. Finally, in this second part of the book, I encapsulate what has been learned in productivity improvement programs work. The material in the second part presents the essence of what I am advising companies to do.

The third part is Chapter 17: personnel planning. With the rate of change occurring in business today, companies must do personnel planning. A practical method for personnel planning is presented.

The last part is Chapter 18. It contains my feelings about the need for personal values in personnel work.

The original source of much of the material is from the "developmental projects" I have been working on with colleagues in client companies for the past eight years. This work was the most practical form of personnel R&D. The subjects were based upon critical issues faced by client companies. New ideas and practices were evolved by working with the personnel staffs of these firms. Results of this in-company client work then became part of the agenda of conferences I have been holding, on an invitation-only basis, in Florida each year. About sixty top-level personnel professionals attend these conferences each year. Some results have been published in *The Sibson Report*, which is, in fact, a consultative personnel information service.

There is much that is new in this book and different from what is now being practiced in many companies. This should not be viewed as a criticism of what is being done. Different ideas, approaches, and practices have become necessary because of the changes in business and in the work force. I am not embarrassed by the fact that what I recommend now is different from what I recommended before, sometimes only a few years ago. Conditions are changing. Also, personnel is a relatively new field, and we have learned from our experiences.

I have been doing personnel work for thirty-five years; so much of what I was taught in graduate business school and practiced in the early 1950s is clearly obsolete and inappropriate today. It's not that we were wrong then and right now, but rather that we were mostly right then and now.

In the chapter on the personnel department, I describe the four phases of the evolution of the personnel function. I have worked during three of them. A great deal has, indeed, changed in personnel in only thirty-five years.

But *only* thirty-five years ago Harry Truman was president; North Korea invaded South Korea; we had not yet developed the hydrogen bomb; the United Nations Building in New York City had just been completed; the population of the United States had just passed 150 million; there were only one and a half million TV sets in this country (black and white, of course); and one of the most popular songs was "If I Knew You Were Comin' I'd've Baked a Cake." The principal plane used for business flights was the DC-3; the biggest computer in the world couldn't match the PCjr; and we all used slide rules. Sally Sibson was Sally Wallace, a senior at Roxborough High School in Philadelphia.

No one particularly likes change. Certainly in business, we would prefer to do what we know, in a way that worked well in the past. But with the world changing around us and at an accelerating rate, much of what worked well before in personnel won't work now.

A couple of years ago, as the keynote speaker at an American Compensation Association· meeting in Phoenix, I gave my last personnel speech. Now I have written my last of seven personnel books. For Sally and me, it has been a labor of love and we have done our very best. For you, we hope there is value.

Robert E. Sibson

Vero Beach, Florida
Summer 1984

The Management of Personnel

Chapter 1

MANAGEMENT AND PERSONNEL

If Andrew Carnegie was correct in the 1920s when he said that "people are our most important assets," then it may be equally correct to say today that *people are our only assets.* With an enormous increase and a growing diversity of knowledge jobs, those who work in the enterprise are increasingly becoming unique assets. The excellence of the management of personnel is then a critical executive skill. In some firms improving the management of personnel is a high-priority need. In other firms, improving the excellence of the management of personnel represents a major business opportunity.

OUR HUMAN RESOURCES

There was a time when our country had many unique economic assets, and we were clearly number one. We produced much of the world's oil and more than our share of many other basic resources. We had advanced technology not possessed by others. We had by far the most knowledgeable, skilled, resourceful, and productive work force in the world.

Our nation still has many resources. We still have a great deal of oil—enough to supply all our needs for a while, provided everyone were to drive a compact car. Before many years, however, we will have to find a substitute for oil and many other basic resources. We are using up many of our basic resources, and we will have to develop new resources. It is our workers who must invent, develop, and deliver these substitute basic resources.

1

We have great agricultural resources. But we don't have more farmland or even better farmland than others. We have more effective farmers. We also need more effective operators in the industrial and service sectors of our economy if we are to compete effectively in international markets.

As a nation, we still have great people assets. American workers are educated, trained, and motivated. The work ethic still lives; it isn't dead yet. Most workers want to do their best, or at least they want to do well; and workers know that they have to pay their bills. Most of those who work have pride in their work or want to have pride in their work. There is still a great deal of "American ingenuity." Our people assets are still high, perhaps the highest in the world. But our people assets and employee productivity are eroding, and increasingly they are being challenged by workers in other nations.

There is ample data to prove that productivity has declined in this country during the past ten years. In many firms, if not all firms, people assets—the level of knowledge and skill—are not increasing as much as they should. Increasing the human asset base and increasing the effectiveness of work must be done at the individual enterprise level, and they must be done by those who do the work as well as by those who manage the work.

Certainly, the government can help. The government can help by establishing economic policies that promote greater productivity, by implementing fiscal and tax policies that encourage necessary investment, by being even-handed in the administration of laws affecting business, and by being reasonable in balancing the needs for increasing the effectiveness of work against other social objectives. In fact, to compete in world markets today, the government and business must be partners and not adversaries.

The government can help, but companies and the people who work in companies must do it. Executives can't do it alone. Executive management must set the policies and the work environment that are more conducive to effective work. Workers and operating managers at every level are the ones who will (or will not) increase the effectiveness of work.

MANAGEMENT OF THE WORK FORCE

Effective management of the work force must start with a conviction by those who manage the firm that those who work in the firm are truly critical to the success of the business. Executive management must be convinced that the human resources of the firm are critical resources and that high levels of work effectiveness are critical to the success of the firm. Executive management must have confidence that the effectiveness of the work of people in the firm can be substantially improved through greater excellence of management.

In the past, executives in most firms thought that productivity was good enough; that the work force was capable enough. Only in recent years has productivity improvement become a high-priority item in many firms. Generally, productivity improvement has occurred in companies where there was a commitment to take actions and implement programs to increase the human asset base and to increase the effectiveness of work.

Management, the management of people, and the supervision of subordinate work have been thought of and treated as the same thing; and probably that was the case not many years ago. Today, there are many who manage assets or knowledge but not people. The management of people doesn't need to be done and cannot always be done by everyone who supervises the work of others.

The management of personnel involves the authority and responsibility for substantive decisions about people at work, employment decisions, selection for promotion, organizational structuring decisions, job structuring, training and development, communications of policies, and other important company matters. Many who assign tasks, instruct, review the technical excellence of work, schedule work, and perform other operational tasks lack personnel knowledge, management experience, and the required skills to perform the tasks outlined, all of which reflect the true *management* of personnel.

The management of personnel thus requires the identification of those who do this management work. For these people, the management of personnel must be a major part of what they do, and the performance of these managers must be evaluated by how well the people who are managed do their work, just as a football

3

coach is evaluated by how well the players perform and, ultimately, their win-loss record.

Rarely do managers of personnel spend their full time managing personnel. As individual contributors, they do other things as well. In that respect, they are no different from any other worker. But as important as their individual contributor task may be, the effective management of personnel must be a high-priority responsibility, because this activity can be leveraged into higher effectiveness of work of many other people.

Managers of personnel need to be selected with these thoughts in mind. They must have demonstrated talent and potential in personnel management and personal relations as one essential selection criterion. Once they are on this career path of managing personnel, there must be development—not in cloned behavior or the "company way," but in the skills of managing personnel. Early in this management of personnel career path, development requires mastering such basic matters as interviewing skills and pay planning. Ultimately, such advanced skills as consensus decision making and leadership must be mastered. Given the correct business strategies and proper deployment of assets, the company with excellence in management of personnel is the firm that, over time, will most likely emerge as the best and the most successful. This is the inevitable conclusion of the assumption that people are our most important assets. Managers must know how to manage people, and the people must strive to do their best. That is the winning game plan in any enterprise.

ARE EMPLOYEES DOING THEIR BEST?

In a rather homespun manner, the April 1981 issue of *The Sibson Report* commented on whether employees were doing their best and whether the excellence of management of personnel was good enough. That report said:

When our Vero Beach High School Fighting Indians football team won the Florida State Championship at the Citrus Bowl this year, the local TV commentator introduced the taped highlights of the game by saying:

It took a bunch of kids who wanted to do it, and a coach who knew how to do it.

It struck us that in those 20 words is *the* formula for the success of *every* large corporation.

You need to have employees who want to do it. Management must know how to do it.

Do your employees want to do it? Does your management know how to do it? Is your company a "winner"?

Generally, employees in this country are doing less than their best work. They don't want to do poorly, but increasingly they aren't inclined to do their best. Most work hard, frequently under difficult conditions. For many, work is also boring; for some, conditions of work range necessarily from unpleasant to unsafe. Nevertheless, the fact is that most employees are not doing well enough; all employees need to do *their best.*

In personnel work today, we need to deal with some very basic issues. One of these is exactly what we mean by "their best." For some employees, working more effectively means working harder. Harder isn't necessarily more arduous or even more distasteful. Frequently it's just adjusting to a different pace of work. Sometimes it's only a matter of not wasting time. Occasionally it may mean developing good work habits.

Sometimes "their best" means working "smarter." "Working smarter" doesn't necessarily mean working more intelligently. It may mean doing the things that are most relevant. It may mean doing things in a simpler manner. You may work smarter by doing things in the right order, by setting the right priorities.

How do we know that employees are not now doing their best work? They tell us they aren't. For over thirty years I have asked groups of employees, on hundreds of occasions, whether they were doing their best. In every case, the answer was a simple and honest "no." Groups of supervisors were asked the same question about their subordinates, and they too, without exception, thought that those who worked for them worked less than their best. If you have any doubts, ask your employees. Ask yourself if you are really doing your very best. Ask yourself if your peers and your bosses are doing their best. The answer is almost always the same—not really.

How much less than their best are employees working? There is no specific data to answer that question. But every group of employees I ever discussed this with said they thought that they could work 20 to 30 percent more effectively than they were now working.

Why are employees doing less than their best? Why don't they want to be winners? Surely they don't want to be losers. They don't want to have real earnings decline, to be laid off, to be involved in "give-backs," or to see their jobs exported to Taiwan. The work ethic still lives, but it is waning and may be ailing, though it is not yet terminally ill.

There are many reasons why employees generally are doing less than their best. Some of the reasons most frequently identified when this subject is openly discussed with employees include the following:

1. Many employees don't really think that "it's their game." They really don't feel that they are part of the company. The "them and us" feeling is becoming more importantly a part of the American workers' attitude and is detracting from their effectiveness of work.

2. Employees don't always feel that, as individuals or as a group, what they do or how well they do it makes a difference. This is analogous to the feelings of many voters who don't vote because they feel that one vote doesn't make any difference. It is only partially a result of the growing scale of size in American busineses.

3. Many employees will tell you that they are often prevented from doing their best. They must follow the established procedures or work the company's way, even when that means they work inefficiently or to poor quality standards. If they *can't* do their best with respect to some activities, they likely *won't* do their best with respect to other activities.

4. Employees think that excellence is not always rewarded and is usually not rewarded sufficiently. Surveys of personnel professionals and business executives show that they too think that excellence is not sufficiently rewarded. Many employees try to do their best anyway. But when mediocrity is rewarded about as much excellence, it takes away some of the drive for excellence.

5. Over the past few decades, workers have been lulled into thinking that they don't have to do their best; that we can all be successful by doing less than our best. They have been led to believe this by the government, by the media, by labor leaders, and by some managers in their own companies. Work is not so pleasant for most people that the work ethic will thrive unless workers think that effective work is important.

6. The level of hunger is in inverse proportion to the degree to which the stomach is full. Similarly, there is a relationship between ambition and striving for excellence on the one hand and the standard of living on the other. In other words, the very fact that this country has achieved high standards of living has dulled some workers' desire to do their best.

There are other reasons why workers, in specific cases, do less than their best. The list above, however, is sufficient to result in substantially less than optimum work effectiveness. At the bottom line of these factors must be inadequacies in the management of personnel, or—to look at it in a positive way—a substantial opportunity to improve business results through more effective management of personnel.

A NEED FOR IMPROVED EFFECTIVENESS IN THE MANAGEMENT OF PERSONNEL

The most important single reason why there is a need to improve the excellence of managing personnel is because the number of knowledge workers has increased sevenfold over the past twenty-five years; it is increasing at this rate today, and that rate of increase will continue. Furthermore, in the future, the diversity of knowledge jobs will continue to increase dramatically. If these forecasts are correct, then the annual rate of increase in the number of knowledge workers will be 7.5 percent per year in the foreseeable future, and there will be a 3 percent increase in the number of knowledge jobs in the work force each year.

This change in the work force represents major challenges in the management of personnel. Many of these knowledge positions involve highly technical matters that cannot be managed in traditional ways. To a large extent, many knowledge workers determine their own work methods and, in many cases, what work is to be done and the order in which it is to be done.

There are also more people today who must be managers of personnel. The work force has grown considerably. This growth and the increasing diversity of positions have resulted in a decrease in the ratio of supervised persons to supervisors. Twenty years ago, the ratio of supervised to supervisors was more than seven to one among salaried workers and triple that amount for operations workers. Today, those ratios are about half what they used to be. This means that there are far more people who are making personnel decisions, and this makes the effective application of personnel programs more difficult.

Supervisors are also more disparate in the nature of work they do and their backgrounds. Managers of personnel are frequently dispersed geographically. Under these circumstances, traditional personnel practices work less effectively than they did a few years ago.

For many who manage personnel in contemporary business, supervision is a secondary or tertiary activity. Many do not really have a manageable amount of time to manage personnel because they have so few subordinates. Some lack the skills, the experience, and the knowledge to do the management of personnel job effectively.

In fact, many supervisors today are disinclined to spend the time, and many are not motivated to achieve excellence in the management of personnel. Not everyone wants to be a field commander or even a platoon leader. Today, in fact, many who have responsibility for managing personnel are more oriented toward the technical or administrative aspects of their work and think of their professional discipline as their first priority.

Many who supervise personnel today, as well as those who are supervised, are also disinclined to accept great numbers of rules and procedures. Because of the size and diversity of business as well as the technical nature of the jobs involved, more people have a greater opportunity to disregard established rules. This also weakens what has essentially been a proceduralized and programmatic style of managing personnel from a centralized location.

Furthermore, there are new elements in the management of people. For instance, different supervisory relationships are emerging. The level of technology and the highly specialized administrative skills of an increasing number of people are such that supervision is increasingly less in the manner of directing and controlling the work that is done. There are some highly professional positions where the nature of supervision today is more in the mode of a "homeroom teacher."

Various types of project work are also increasing. Because of this, many individuals will have a number of "supervisors" in the course of a year, each directing or impacting in some way what the individual does, the results which are expected, and, to some extent, the work done. Each of these project supervisors has some impact on how the person does the work and some view of his performance. Each project supervisor, therefore, has something to contribute to the management of each person. In modern business, this way of working also makes it increasingly difficult to have a proceduralized or programmatic system of management or management of personnel on a highly centralized basis.

Because of such changing conditions of work, basic principles of the management of personnel that were correct and useful only a few years ago have little or no validity today. Examples would include such longstanding ideas as appropriate span of control and the traditional notion of "one person/one manager." Some traditional administrative techniques of managing people are also becoming increasingly obsolete or more difficult to implement. This includes job evaluation and programmatic training. The perpetuation of antiquated practices detracts from the effec-

9

tiveness of managing personnel. New techniques and new practices that are more consistent with the needs of business today have evolved and are described in this book.

EVOLUTION OF MORE EFFECTIVE METHODS
OF MANAGING PERSONNEL

Firms need to evolve their management-of-personnel method from what has largely been a programmatic approach to a "delegative method" of managing personnel. What has been labeled the "delegative method" of managing personnel is a style or process of management, not a program. This style is not "new"—as in the sense of an invention. Nor is the delegative method totally different from what companies do now. But it has differences in approach, emphasis, and methodology, which require changes in managing people, restructuring or abandoning some practices, and developing new personnel practices and techniques.

This is not the first time that business has had to change basic methods of managing personnel. If we go back far enough in the history of business, the basic style of managing personnel was highly *autocratic*. During the early periods of economic development, most workers were artisans, individual businessmen, or farmers. The number of employees were few, and typically the enterprises they worked in were rather small. The managers were also the owners, and they had absolute economic decision-making power. In a sense, employees were considered to be property, and this style of management flourished when property rights transcended all other rights.

The autocratic style of managing people lasted for hundreds of years, but by the 1800s it was replaced by what can be labeled the *discretionary* style of management. Like all basic changes in complex social systems, the change to a discretionary style of managing personnel was not caused by a single event or by one force alone.

As businesses grew, for example, autocratic owners had to hire subordinate managers and were disinclined to have employee/managers wield the same autocratic authority as they exercised. There was also public revulsion against some employer

10

practices under the autocratic management style. Most of all, as the number of employees grew, the number of employee voters grew also, and in the 1800s we saw the emergence of labor laws, which constrained the absolute economic authority of employers.

Under the discretionary system, a number of top executives made personnel decisions on a judgmental basis. These decisions were constrained, however, by an increasing number of laws. Public corporations emerged, and they had boards of directors who also constrained the authority of top managers. Executives had data of various sorts available to assist them in making discretionary judgments.

As businesses continued to grow, this discretionary system of managing personnel developed its own set of problems. With many managers in the organization exercising discretionary decisions, top management found that the result was a form of anarchy. Also, in the early 1900s, as far back as that may seem, the first basic practices of personnel management emerged, particularly with respect to recruiting, pay, and training. Finally, in the 1900s, another force came on the scene: trade unions. And trade unions opposed discretionary authority by managers.

The transition from the discretionary to the programmatic system of managing people occurred over a number of years, but it was in the middle 1930s, when there was mass unionization of industrial workers, that the symbolic transition to the programmatic system of managing personnel took place. By the 1940s, the programmatic system of management dominated as a system of managing people at work. Therefore, the discretionary system lasted but 100 years.

The programmatic system of managing people, it is suggested, is now giving way in the 1980s to a more "delegative method" of managing personnel. The delegative method will be dominant by 1990. Therefore, the programmatic system lasted only about fifty years.

Essentially, the programmatic method relied on programs, rules, and procedures for the management of personnel. Personnel experts developed the "best practices," and supervisors throughout the firm applied those practices in a uniform manner. To a great extent, programs made the decisions, and training programs "cloned" supervisors throughout the firm to apply the practices in the same manner, with the thought that there would then be excellence and consistency.

In describing the programmatic system of managing people, there is no thought of either criticizing or applauding it. It's the method that existed, and it evolved to meet the needs of the time. We have no idea how well it worked, because we have no idea what the alternatives might have been. We do know that it worked better than what preceded it, the discretionary system. We know that it worked much better in the 1940s than in the 1970s, even though we had better programs in the 1970s.

With reflection, it seems that we probably had too many programs. They were too detailed and too rigidly applied. Fewer programs, with less detail and less rigid application, represent the essentials of the "delegative method" of managing personnel.

At no point in time, however, has one method of managing people dominated to the exclusion of others. What's really happened is that the management of people was dominated by one method, but elements of others were present. It's best to illustrate this by identifying each of the basic methods of managing personnel with a color:

- Autocratic—white
- Discretionary—yellow
- Programmatic—red
- Delegative—blue

The change that occurred was from white to pale yellow to deep yellow, from orange to red; and now the change is from red to purple. At any point in time, elements of each style of management may exist. In a company today that has progressed a great deal in the evolution of the delegative method of managing, the actual management practices might be 50 percent delegative, 30 percent programmatic, 15 percent discretionary, and 5 percent autocratic.

THE EFFECTIVENESS OF WORK

There are sufficient existing amounts of knowledge, usable programs, and experiences in personnel management to increase

12

the effectiveness of work substantially. The essential task is to improve the application of the personnel programs that exist, to sharpen and focus existing practices to the needs of the business, and to relate what is known in personnel to each business and to each operation within a business.

Personnel is one of the knowledge areas that has evolved in the past fifty years. Today there are many people in the field. Furthermore, the caliber of those doing the work has increased enormously, and those coming up in the field are usually brighter, better trained, and more able than those of us they are replacing. So there is ample personnel talent, as well as a sufficient amount of personnel experience, to increase the effectiveness of work.

The know-how of operating managers in personnel subjects is also substantial. Not many years ago, most of those who managed people knew little about staffing, training, compensation, and other areas of personnel. But, for some time now, they have been working with and have been affected by programs in all areas of personnel. Many have taken courses in personnel in college, and all are constantly exposed to personnel know-how in the literature of business. Thus, lack of manager know-how seems to be no barrier to greater effectiveness of work.

Senior management is well versed in personnel. Senior managers have made substantial commitments to more effective management of personnel in the past. The size of personnel departments is proof of that. Also, the degree to which top executives in many firms have made some substantial financial and personal time commitments to one personnel fad after another is incredible, but it demonstrates clear executive management support of more effective management of personnel.

The key to increasing the effectiveness of managing people, and thereby substantially increasing the effectiveness of work, involves the will to do it, not just in the sense of a commitment of time and money but rather in terms of a commitment to change.

Our whole society is experiencing an economic revolution that is more pronounced than any in history. The revolution we are experiencing is not dramatic, so we don't feel it at any point in time and are generally unaware that it is happening. Business in general, as well as the way we manage people, is not immune to this revolution.

Someday, historians may describe this revolution we are

experiencing. Sociologists, philosophers, and all the rest don't seem to know what is happening. But this we do know: the impetus of the revolution is technology, and the result is change. And so it is with the management of personnel.

Executives, managers, personnel people, and all of us who work must adapt to change, and we must change our ways. It would be best, more orderly, and less painful if executives led the way. Executives must do more than make the commitment to more effective management of personnel. They must also change *their* ways.

As far as the management of personnel is concerned (and that is the issue here), executives must first disabuse themselves of the notion that they are the company. They are very important paid workers. They are highly valued, quite respected, usually obeyed, and sometimes liked, but they are still paid employees.

With respect to the management of personnel, executives must also realize that they do little of the managing today. Executives really don't like to hear that, but it is the truth. Of course, they are the most important people in the company, and they must do the most important things. They set policy, establish the company culture, determine the styles of management, and make other basic decisions with respect to direction and objectives. But they canot manage everything. They cannot manage people throughout the organization. Their ability to manage personnel is limited to a couple of dozen of their most immediate associates. The role of executives in the management of other personnel is limited to policies, requirements, guidelines, and auditing activities. If executives do anything else in personnel, it is probably not managing but meddling. In the management of personnel, executive management must attend to those matters which they can uniquely achieve; and they must do them very well. Then they must let others manage throughout the firm.

Executives are uncomfortable with this notion. They have concerns, for example, about whether the work will be done well under such a delegative style of managing personnel. That's a real concern, but we know how to deal with it; and required monitoring and auditing activities are covered in this book.

Personnel professionals must change also, focusing on the application of personnel know-how rather than the development of new programs and practices, which was the primary need in the past forty years of the programmatic style of managing personnel. Now and in the future, managers rather than programs are the key to the excellence of the management of personnel. So the focus of personnel professionals is to apply their know-how to support the work of managers, to make them better managers, and to be direct partners in solving people problems or exploiting opportunities to increase productivity.

We don't know how good the managers will be or whether or not all workers (including manager-workers) will do their best. However, we have enough experience to know that the manager will do far better than he has been doing by applying the type of thinking and practices outlined, and, in today's environment, people can be more effectively managed under a delegative style than under a programmatic style.

INCREASING THE EFFECTIVENESS OF WORK

There is a critical need for excellence in the management of personnel. Technology and productivity are the keys to the economic future, the keys to providing jobs for a growing work force, improving real earnings, financing desired social programs, and paying for adequate national security.

The state of our nation seems good, but it's getting less good all the time. Not many years ago the United States was clearly the most powerful, most advanced, and wealthiest of nations. We were clearly number one. It seems that we probably still are number one, but it is far less clear. What is clear is that we are slipping, or others are catching up.

When I was a young man, the inscription "Made in Japan" on an item meant that it was a piece of junk. Today, "Made in USA" too often means that it probably won't work. And, besides that, so much of what was made in the USA isn't made here anymore. Sometimes it appears that our nation's principal export is jobs.

Many great societies in history rose to prominence—to be number one. Ours is just the latest. All before us experienced their zenith, and then started to fall to number two and then to second-rate, and some, given enough time, ceased to exist. The circumstances varied with respect to the demise of each great society, but one characteristic was common to all: decadence. Our country has plainly entered the early stages of a period of decadence.

One element of that decadence in the demise of every great society has been a decline in the effectiveness of work: productivity. In this country, national productivity started the decline in the early 1970s. Technology and the more effective management of personnel are the only ways to cause a reversal of this trend and an upward resurgence in productivity.

There are some, including heads of major corporations, who think there is no hope for more effective management of personnel in the future. They see in the future a continuing decline in the real earnings of working people and continued lower productivity. They see a work force that will turn from questioning to indifference and then to outright hostility. Some predict the end of our enterprise system by the end of the 1990s and the end of our political system in the twenty-first century. Unless there is a quantum leap in improvement in the management of personnel, theirs may be a self-fulfilling prophecy.

Such prophets of doom, however, underrate the American working people, mostly because they don't know them. Working people possess notable skills, knowledge, enterprise, and pride. They want to do an effective job. They are our economic and political franchise. They are our only assets.

Business leaders who doubt that the effectiveness of work can be greatly increased are right if they mean that they—the managers—alone can do it. It is the total human assets of all of the partners—the combined knowledge and capabilities of all our working men and women—that must be enhanced. Those enhanced assets, translated into increased productivity in the broadest sense of that word, will reverse the downward trend in productivity.

Actually, we may be at a critical crossroad. There is reason to hope that, with new technology, our country could improve productivity at an average annual rate of 3 percent for up to thirty-five years. Then the average family's living standard, in real dollars, would *triple*. That's worth going for.

If we are successful in certain critical and basic activities, including substantial improvement in the excellence of the management of personnel, then ours can be the first civilization to reverse a decline and rise again to a new level of growth, strength, and prosperity. Then ours would be the first great society that entered a period of decline to obscurity and experienced a resurgence of progress and achievement to a new and undreamed-of level of economic development. Only that scenario will assure national security and pay the bills for substantial future social progress.

Leadership by management of the still free-enough enterprise system is the only likely source for such a success. With such management leadership, working men and women will do it.

Chapter 2

THE DELEGATIVE METHOD OF MANAGING PERSONNEL

The "delegative method" of managing personnel is a style or process of management, not a program. This style is not new, and it is not totally different from what companies now do. But it is a different approach. It has different methodology and emphasizes decision making at the lowest level. The application of the delegative method will require changes in managing people, restructuring or abandonment of some practices, and development of new personnel practices and techniques.

THE PROGRAMMATIC METHOD
OF MANAGING PERSONNEL

Essentially, most firms today have a programmatic method of managing personnel. Under this style of managing personnel, companies develop programs, practices, and processes in the field of personnel. These are typically developed by personnel experts and reviewed and approved by top management.

Then the programs are implemented. Managers and supervisors throughout the company make key personnel decisions in accordance with the programs. In fact, they are trained to apply the programs "correctly," which generally means "the same way."

In this way, the decisions and thinking of top management are embodied in the personnel programs. If the programs are applied in the correct (same) way by supervisors throughout the

18

organization, top executives' thinking and decisions are carried out throughout the organization.

In effect, under the programmatic method of managing personnel, it is, to a very large degree, the programs that make the decisions. And because the programs make decisions, or highly influence decisions that are made, there is a uniformity to decision-making. This method was supposed to bring consistency, equality, and impartiality into personnel decision making through the organization.

Personnel programs were developed in many areas of the business. Job evaluation, testing, performance evaluation, organizational structuring, and salary guidelines are all examples of the many personnel programs that were developed and programs that made or forced or directed personnel decisions. Programs were improved and made more and more sophisticated. Personnel program development, in fact, was a main activity of personnel professionals for many years.

Personnel programs were complemented by other proceduralized methods. These included policy manuals, which rarely stated policies but rather contained many rules. The rules determined what supervisors did and how they handled various personnel situations. To a very large extent, the rules made the decisions.

The programmatic method was evolved when there were many employees doing relatively few jobs. The jobs were mostly unskilled or semi-skilled. Supervisors of most employees were low level and untrained in management, and they had not learned the various techniques and technology of personnel management.

The difficulties that companies increasingly experienced with the programmatic method led to a more delegative style and greater latitude of action in personnel decision making. No one sat down and invented a new method. A new method has been evolving in hundreds of companies and by thousands of managers to meet the needs of a changing work force and changing business circumstances. These changes were observed, and a conceptual framework was developed to describe what was happening and to assist the evolution to this more effective method of managing personnel.

The evolution of the delegative method of managing personnel as a basic conceptual framework actually evolved over a two-and-a-half–year period of observation and study of personnel programs and their effectiveness in various companies. This study showed clearly that programs being developed were getting better and better, that they were applied by increasingly knowledgeable personnel people and line managers, but that they were working less and less well. There was only one explanation for these seemingly contradictory observations. The problem was in the programs themselves. Doing the wrong things better makes the results worse.

Personnel programs and procedures, as the key to managing personnel, worked less and less well because of the increasing number of jobs, the greater diversity of jobs, and the higher technological content of jobs. Also, business itself was getting more diverse and more complex. There was a whole new generation of managers who knew about personnel management and its various techniques and practices. Under these circumstances, programs that answered personnel questions simply could not work as well as needed for effective management of the work force.

Let's use job evaluation as an example. Job evaluation was always based upon job knowledge. Job knowledge, recorded in a job description, was evaluated by experts, usually at a central location, against a job evaluation plan or program. It was the plan or program (correctly applied) that determined salary level. That whole system, however, depended upon job knowledge, which, in turn, depended upon the ability of someone to write a job description. Today there are increasing numbers of jobs that cannot be described, and job evaluation experts who don't know the jobs don't really understand what work is being done. Furthermore, because of the increasing number, diversity, and technical content of jobs, job evaluation programs measure some jobs better than others, and some jobs are not measured adequately. This is the problem, in varying degrees, with all personnel programs and rules.

Knowledge of the work done is critical in the management of personnel today. The knowledge of people who do the work is essential. Personnel decisions based upon knowledge of the work and knowledge of the people can only be made by those in the organization who know the jobs and the people. The delegative approach is designed around these realities of the contemporary business.

THE DELEGATIVE METHOD

The delegative method of managing personnel has four essential interrelated elements:

• Policy management
• Guideline management
• Delegative practices
• Quality management

Policy management sets the objectives and describes the thinking of top management. Policy management is the foundation of the management of personnel, a foundation determined personally by top executives.

Guideline management establishes a few requirements. These are set only when they are required by law or when essential corporate matters are involved. Essentially, under guideline management, guides, along with information and consultative services by the personnel department, provide references to be used by managers throughout the organization in making personnel decisions.

Delegative practices are the vital organ in the systems method of managing personnel. Delegative practices refer to whatever is done to vest in managers throughout the organization, who know the work and the people who do the work, the authority and accountability for making personnel decisions, and, in turn, these practices, make possible the delegation of some decisions to the workers about how they do their work.

Quality management is a system of review, monitoring, analysis, and audits to ensure that the management of personnel is consistent with policies, conforms to requirements, reflects guidelines, and contributes to the effectiveness of work. Quality management is so named because its purpose is to ensure a high quality of decision making throughout the organization.

Each of these basic elements exists in personnel management today. What's different under the delegative method are the format and the emphasis. Most important, under the delegative approach, programs are rarely the essential decision-making process.

Each of the four elements of the delegative method is designed to delegate decision making to managers throughout the organization. In today's business environment, the assumption of this approach is that personnel decisions must be made by those who understand the technology of the work, the jobs being performed, and the people doing the work. You can't have delegative management, however, without quality management; top executives must be assured that the job being delegated is being done well.

The transition from a proceduralized or programmatic approach of managing personnel to a delegative method is not technically difficult, but it involves change. Such basic changes inevitably cause concerns, and new and fundamentally different personnel techniques are involved. Furthermore, in this transition, companies are not being forced to change to a new method of management of personnel by unions, or the government, or anyone else. Self-initiated change in the absence of clear and compelling needs is very difficult to accomplish. Technically, however, a company can work through the transitional steps from a programmatic system of managing personnel to a delegative approach within six months. This positions them in the delegative method or style of managing personnel. Then, improvements or refinements in the system can be made in an orderly manner as needs demonstrate. The cost or expense of the transition is very little.

POLICY MANAGEMENT

The term "policy management" has been coined to differentiate it from traditional policies written in business. Policies, as they have existed in personnel, have been quite broad. They have typically been general statements of philosophy, conscience, or broad objectives. Policy management goes further than this. Policy management contains, in sufficient detail to be usable, the explicit thinking and objectives of the top management of the firm. Policy management is the building block upon which the delegative approach to the management of personnel is built.

Need For Policy Management: Policy management, as described here, is needed to assure that policies under a delegative style of managing personnel are set by top executives rather than being determined, in fact, by many lower-level managers. The very broad and general policies that have characterized personnel may have been sufficient under a programmatic approach to the management of personnel. The programs themselves were specific, and therefore top management assured that their intentions were carried out by reviewing and approving these detailed programs, as well as the rules and prescribed practices which were characteristic of a programmatic style.

Actually, even under a programmatic style, there is now a considerable amount of policy setting from the bottom up. In large firms, many hundreds of managers are applying, and to some degree interpreting and explaining, actions under programs that already exist. Over time, their application may reflect something quite different from what was intended by top management. Also, personnel professionals are making technical decisions, and these, in fact, may result in a policy that is different from the policy intended. For example, a firm may have a policy to set pay at market average, but it is the professionals in personnel who collect and interpret the data, and in the process, pay levels compared to the market may actually be very different than intended.

When, as a matter of managerial style, a firm moves to a delegative method, then, by design, managers and personnel professionals have even greater latitude in their decisions. Under these circumstances, policies must be clear and the intentions of top management understandable. Otherwise, policy will be not be determined by top management but by hundreds of lower-level managers throughout the company. Policy management is, therefore, a vital part of the delegative style of managing personnel.

The first objective of policy management is to place policy

making back where it belongs: with executive management. The purpose of policy management is also to ensure that the most appropriate policies are evolved, consistent not only with the company as it exists but also with the strategic plans of the company for changing the business.

Requirements of Policies: To accomplish these objectives, policy management statements must be specific enough to meet very definite criteria. For one thing, the statements must be specific enough so that they are a primary input to personnel staff specialists for designing required programs and practices. The starting points for the design of programs are: the business needs that have been demonstrated, the characteristics of the firm, and *policy management*.

Policy management must also be specific enough to serve as a screen. When salespersons or advocates come forth with recommended answers, policy statements must be a basis for determining whether such activities should be further considered. Policy management is an initial screen; if what is proposed is not consistent with policy management statements, then it is not considered further, regardless of its features or its alleged virtues.

Policy management must also be a basis by which managers throughout the organization make specific decisions and judgments in the field of managing personnel. The various policy statements must also serve as one basis for reviewing the performance of managers and how well they are managing personnel.

Finally, policy management must be specific enough and comprehensive enough so that it becomes an important communications tool. Policy management goes further than simply saying such things, as "pay will be competitive and fair." Policy management statements are specific enough so that people have some understanding of what those words mean.

Written statements of policy alone will not accomplish these objectives. You don't really achieve the goal of policy management by merely writing more words or even more specific words. The statements of policies are more detailed and longer under policy management, but they are only part of the overall policy management system. There are also supplements that are part of policy management. Supplements would include information and data that help people to understand some policies better when making decisions. Supplements may set expectations; for example, expected distribution of performance ratings. Most important, supplements include written precedents and cases. These cases are usually key events in which a specific decision has been made that further describes and illustrates a key policy issue.

In some cases there may be another element of policy management. This would involve the development of models. The models may be in a number of forms; one may simply be a description of some ideal toward which the company is striving.

Developing Written Policy-Management Statements: You don't need to cover a great number of items to achieve the goals of policy management. In all areas of personnel in most large corporations, a dozen management statements may be sufficient. Deal only with true policy issues. Also, deal only with critical issues, issues that are critical to the success of the company and to the welfare of employees. Finally, deal only with subjects where it is possible to detail top management's thinking in a manner that would be applicable throughout the firm.

Considerable art, as well as know-how, is required to develop policy-management statements that meet the requirements that have been outlined. This work must be done by high-level personnel professionals. My advice would be to select one or a few items first. These should be the issues of greatest importance to the firm at the time. Then, sit down and develop specific questions that deal with these items, avoiding open-ended questions or discussions of philosophy. One of the most important skills of the personnel staff is to know what the questions are.

Questions should be subject to a "this-or-that" type of answer, virtually multiple-choice questions. In some cases, present management with a "target answer," a statement that the personnel professional thinks is reasonable but that is designed to get specific responses. The very criticisms and reactions—positive and negative—by top management are the kind of input needed to evolve policy-management statements. It is the sort of specificity that will get top management thinking and talking. Then the job of the personnel professional is to listen. Listening is the second critical skill of the personnel professional.

The personnel professional should prepare a written statement based upon what he heard. This isn't the statement of policy of the personnel professional, but rather what that individual heard top management say: the policy statement that best reflects top management's thinking on the issues discussed.

Some rework will be necessary after top management reacts to that specific written version of their thinking. At this time, also prepare any essential supplements. It's best to prepare as few as possible. Don't make up supplements until you're sure they are needed. There will be no policy-statement precedents at this point. Only later, when questions or critical issues arise, would there be supplemental cases.

GUIDELINE MANAGEMENT

Guideline management is the second integral part of the "delegative method" of managing personnel. It has been called guideline management because it involves a series of practices and programs whose essential purpose is to guide managers in making appropriate personnel decisions. Guideline management is the essential link between policy-management statements and delegative practices, where the actual decisions are delegated to operating managers throughout the organization. The guidelines themselves are developed by the personnel professionals. There are basically three types of guidelines under guideline management. These involve requirements, guides, and information support.

Requirements: Requirements are the leftovers of the programmatic system of managing personnel. They are programs and rules that must be adhered to and followed in a prescribed manner. Under the delegative approach, there are relatively few requirements. But there must also be a very high degree of organizational discipline with respect to these requirements. This is consistent with the trend toward "loose/tight" styles of management.

Exactly which requirements will be established in any firm is obviously a matter highly customized to each business. However, examples of requirements would include such matters as:

- One corporate salary structure must be applied to all businesses and all locations.

- The corporate compensation department will benchmark selected positions by pricing them in the marketplace and assign these jobs to salary grades in the salary structure. These may not be changed anywhere in the organization.

- Performance and potential ratings will be made by all managers on a one-to-five gradient system, and the results of these ratings will be sent to the corporate office.

- There are certain requirements as to "personnel accounting"— for the purposes of the corporate human resources information system.

- There is a prescribed training session that must be attended by all managers of personnel, outlining and describing personnel policy-management statements.

Guides: Guides are, in effect, rules, practices, or programs that are *recommended* by the personnel department. The only requirement is that managers consider these guides, but they do not have to apply them. In effect, the guides reflect the best professional thinking of those in the personnel organization; but they are only there for reference, and line managers in each section and unit of the company may decide whether they will follow these guides and, if so, how they will be applied.

Again, the guides must be customized to the company's situation. Examples of guides that have been used in firms are:

- Management bonus and long-term income plan eligibility guides.

- Interview process recommendations and structured interview form guides.

- Salary increase budgets.

- An approved list of personnel consultants.

Information and Consultative Services: Under the delegative method of managing personnel, the principal activity of the personnel department at corporate and division levels is to accumulate the best knowledge available and make it accessible to all those in the organization. Personnel staff specialists adopt a consultative mode. The information and consultative services, in other words, represent a resource that the corporation has made available to operating managers and first-levels of personnel management.

The following are examples of information and consultative services that have been provided by firms that have moved to the delegative method of managing personnel:

- An internal placement service is available from the corporate office.

- The corporate office provides periodic information briefs and data which they gather in conducting surveys.

- There is a computerized information bank of personnel data.

- Personnel professional development programs are available.

DELEGATIVE PRACTICES

Delegative practices represent a basic management method; it is a style of management. Delegative practices give authority to operating managers throughout the organization to make personnel decisions. These must be within policies and requirements, and reflect consideration of guides. In exercising their authority, managers have information and consultative services available. But the decisions rest with the operating managers charged with the management of personnel.

The Workers: Actually, under the delegative style of management, considerable authority is granted to the workers themselves. A delegative-practices style makes it an integral part of everybody's job to think about, develop, and initiate better work methods. Delegative practices expect workers to do more planning of their own work in order to set correct priorities and do proper scheduling. Delegative practices also assign to each individual the primary job of ensuring a high quality of work. Finally, under the delegative-management system, it is an essential responsibility of each employee to be sure that what he does will not disrupt the work of others. Similarly, workers have a responsibility to communicate actions which are taken by others that are disruptive to their own work.

Under the delegative style of managing, all workers and each group of workers also have areas where they effectively recommend important matters that affect their work. For example, workers would make organizational recommendations, particularly where groups of workers are involved. Workers would make recommendations about roadblocks to effective work and how they might be removed. Workers would make recommendations about communications that would contribute to more effective work.

This essential worker involvement may take many forms. The most widely known of these is quality circles. The specific approach should reflect your company culture, and it should be the approach most comfortable for management. The critical thing is worker involvement, workers making decisions and recommendations about what they know best.

Work is delegated to the workers, but there is no abdication of responsibility. This is not a free-form society. The goal is greater worker initiative, not anarchy in work. Latitude is never complete. Latitude is always restricted, for example, by the work that must be done, some prescribed requirements and methods, safety standards, available equipment, existing facilities, and the decisions of the managers of these workers. It is the supervising manager at every level of the organization who delegates latitude to workers under the delegative-practices style. There is no change in the manager's responsibility to manage, only an expectation as to how that responsibility will be carried out. Therefore, there is no basic change in the nature of the manager's job of managing personnel. What usually happens is that the manager tends to evolve a broader managerial scope in his own work by delegating important matters to those who do the work.

To some extent, responsibility and authority in businesses have been delegated for a very long time. Delegative practices simply extend the art of delegation by assigning more responsibility for development and implementation of better work methods to those who do the work. It is obviously difficult to describe delegative practices in detail, because it is a management style and not a program. There are not necessarily special techniques, meetings, forms, or set procedures.

The Managers: The authority for making personnel decisions is delegated from one level of manager to the next. The goal of delegative management is to have these decisions made at as low a level in the organization as possible. It is in this way that decisions are made by those managers who know the technology, the work, and the workers.

Essentially, where there are delegative practices, the accountability and authority for making personnel decisions has shifted very greatly from programs and rules to the manager of personnel. Remember that it is not a total change; it is a movement from "red" to "purple."

The individual with specific responsibility for managing employees is the center of responsibility in delegative management. Policy-management statements are written to reflect executive management's thinking, not just so that executive management can exercise their rights but as a basic means of making it possible for operating managers to do their job of making personnel decisions more effectively. In addition, requirements, guides, information, and consultative services are all structured and designed to help the operating manager make better personnel decisions. The whole purpose is to facilitate greater effectiveness of work; to increase the productivity of the work force.

Implementing Delegative Practices: Because delegative management is a style of management, it works because that's the way managers run the company at every level of the organization. Just as managers expect people to come to work, under delegative management, they expect employees to seek better methods of doing work and to think "quality." Managers not only let people evolve better ways of doing the work, but they encourage them to do so, and they evaluate their performances, in part, by how well each person develops and carries out work practices that increase productivity and enhance quality.

So it is now *really* a part of the managing supervisor's job to make personnel decisions. It is essential that he is not just assigned that task in a formal manner, but given the time, the authority to do the job, and the support necessary to get the job done.

Delegative management can happen because higher-level managers stop making decisions that can be made at lower levels in the organization. Then personnel decisions are made better and at a lower cost. There is also more time available for higher-level managers to do work that only they can perform.

There are a number of methods that have been used that facilitate delegative practices. Obviously, a company that moves in this direction must evaluate its current managers to make sure that they have the capability and the willingness to assume the authority that will be delegated to them. Some organizational changes may facilitate the evolution of delegative practices. Delegative practices may be applied in one division at a time or in one functional area at a time. This style of management may be evolved by personnel program reviews. A special effort, such as quality circles work, may get the process working. Each method of implementation has worked. But there are two keys: first, there must be the will to do it; second, executive management must start the delegative process by delegating to others.

You will experience some problems when implementing delegative practices. Much of the knowledge about what is really happening with respect to the management of personnel will not be apparent to higher-level managers, and they can experience discomfort with such a situation. The only thing that higher-level management knows is that the effectiveness of work increases and bottom-line results improve.

People's jobs and their roles change when a company moves to a delegative style of managing personnel, and this is not always popular. Not all managers want to assume more authority; some may want too much. The job of the personnel professional also changes dramatically. Managers are not lined up at their doors waiting for decisions from the key personnel people. Those personnel people are now more consultants than program administrators. Some may see this as a diminution of their power, even though their value and their salary grade may increase.

But the values from delegative management are enormous, so the problems are worth the trouble. The values are in a more effective work force. The values involve a more committed work force, a revitalization of the work ethic. The values also involve freeing the time of higher-level management to do things that are critical to the enterprise.

QUALITY MANAGEMENT

Quality management involves those activities, generally carried out by the personnel department, that review, monitor, analyze, and audit the personnel actions and decisions of managers throughout the organization. Quality management is a system to ensure that the management of personnel throughout the organization is consistent with the policy guides of top management, meets requirements that have been established to fulfill corporate needs, reflects guides which are available, and that resources have been properly utilized by supervising managers. Thus quality management is concerned with the quality of personnel decisions that have been delegated to supervisory management throughout the organization under the delegative method of managing personnel.

The quality of personnel decisions and the effectiveness of work have, of course, always been vital to business success. Under a programmatic method of managing personnel, however, the emphasis on quality was to develop the correct programs in the first place, and then to ensure that supervisory managers applied these correct programs the same way. To the extent that there are still some programs in a delegative method of managing personnel, then this practice still represents one element of quality management. Where there are delegative practices, then the quality control over personnel actions is some after-the-fact form of quality management.

Each firm will have to evolve its own quality management

activities. Increasingly, however, a firm will necessarily rely more and more on the following techniques of quality management:

- Personnel reviews
- Monitoring methods
- Comparative analysis techniques
- Personnel audits

Personnel Reviews: Personnel reviews involve examinations of a key area or activity, on a nonscheduled need or interest basis. These reviews would generally be conducted by a firm's own personnel staff, though in special areas, such as executive pay, outside consultants might be used. There is a variety of personnel reviews that might be conducted. A few examples will illustrate their nature and their purpose.

When designing any new program or practice, it's always a good idea to identify a time and a method for subsequent review, which would indicate the degree to which the new activity has achieved its objectives. When this is done, it represents a personnel review. If there is no prescribed method of review identified at the time the new activity is developed, a review can be designed and conducted later.

Personnel reviews may simply be a part of visits to a location by high-level personnel people for some other purpose. Such reviews may be conducted between other meetings or at lunch. They may be informal, and the primary objective may be to make suggestions or to pass on the experiences of other locations that might be helpful. In the process of this highly positive and contributive type of session, the high-level person would be getting a sense of the quality of the management of personnel.

An example of a different type of personnel review is the examination of success cases. One location may have demonstrated particular excellence in some area of personnel management. The practices used at that location can then be examined to see if there are lessons to be learned that would be of use to other units in the organization. Again, the first objective is positive and contributive; an important by-product is additional input to gauging the quality of the management of personnel in various locations.

On occasion, senior management may want some specific area reviewed. This may be because of some visible problem or tangible concern or as part of a normal management review of critical areas of particular concern to senior management. The questions would be investigated and answered, and this part of the review would be investigative and technical. But, in these activities, related issues are inevitably examined and discussed, which provide additional insight into the quality of the management of personnel and leads to concrete suggestions for improvement.

These are only illustrations of personnel reviews. We would be in utopia if this were the only form of a quality management practice that had to be utilized. However, personnel reviews should be the heart of quality management, and additional activities should be designed and utilized as experience demonstrates they are required. Because personnel reviews are essentially positive and contributive, and because they involve moderate amounts of incremental time and cost, they represent virtually a zero-cost element of quality management.

Monitoring and Comparative Analysis: Corporate personnel should have an ongoing information monitoring system that would be an integral part of the quality management activity. Each level of the personnel organization—not just the corporate personnel department—would have information monitoring systems. All of these should be integrated, in the same sense (but not to same degree) that there are consistent charts of accounts and reporting systems in accounting. These information monitoring systems should be a part of the company's human resources information system, and a principal purpose of the HRIS is that it is a system of monitoring the quality of personnel management throughout the organization.

Comparative analysis is an extension of information monitoring. It involves analysis of information. One location's experience may be compared with other locations' experiences with respect to key personnel activities. Analysis may compare current activities with prior results or with pre-set standards, goals, or models. It is now also possible to conduct intercompany comparative analyses.

Comparative analysis can be done now, but its use as a decision-making tool and as an element of quality management will grow enormously as the information revolution continues. Currently, the potential of comparative analysis is for information which only can be viewed and then judgments made as to the significance of the information and what, if anything, should be done about it. Before long (maybe next year) there will also be some capacity for the information system itself to indicate the significance of some information and indicate possible corrective actions.

Monitoring activities and comparative analyses will flow primarily to the corporate office. However, some of that information will also be fed to the supervisory managers, assisting them to become more effective in the management of personnel. Thus the monitoring and comparative analysis activities are an integral part of the quality management system, but they also contribute to more effective management of personnel.

The Personnel Audit: The last, and by far the most formal, part of the quality management activity involves personnel audits. A personnel audit is a formal and rather comprehensive investigation of personnel management in a section of the company. Such audits are not legal requirements but a management-initiated part of quality management. As a result, such audits need not be made each year; in fact, they need be made only once every three to five years, depending in part on the results of the prior audit.

As part of a quality management program within the delegative method of managing personnel, personnel audits would first determine the extent to which personnel management was conducted in compliance with policy management. The audit would also specifically check to make sure that existing requirements were being carried out as prescribed. In these two areas, the personnel audit is detailed and extensive, and it is similar to financial audits.

Personnel audits look also at how much and how well supervisory managers and location personnel people utilize guides and support services. In these areas, the auditors are only sampling experiences and judging how well available resources are being utilized. This phase of the personnel audit is highly diagnostic, much like an annual physical. The auditor examines key symptomatic areas of critical nature in the management of personnel. Depending upon the initial information, the auditor is either satisfied with that area or probes further.

Personnel audits must be conducted by high-level and very experienced people. Audits take time; as a rule of thumb, one day's time by the auditor for each five hundred employees at a location. The results are a formal assessment of the quality of the management of personnel, with conclusions as to how the management of people should be improved and changed.

Personnel professionals must conduct these audits because the auditors are looking at technical matters, and much of their assessment must be based not only on their knowledge of the field of personnel but their extensive experience and the precedents that only experience can provide. But the personnel professional is conducting the audit for executive management, just as the public accountant conducts a financial audit for executive management.

The personnel audit is the anchor or the final test of the quality and effectiveness of personnel management throughout the organization. It is a new activity, which, no doubt, will be done better with time and experience. Enough is known now, however, about how to conduct a personnel audit, and these audits are an indispensable part of quality management.

Chapter 3

THE MANAGERS OF PERSONNEL

In dealing with matters of managing personnel, it is important to give some attention to the question of who the managers are, as well as the basic style by which they manage. The obvious answer to the question of who manages personnel might be all those who have employee subordinates. Increasingly, however, this is not necessarily the correct answer; it is often overly simplistic and not workable, at least in parts of every company of substantial size.

THE TRADITION OF MANAGEMENT

Traditionally, everyone who had subordinates managed people and was a manager of personnel. If you took that traditional definition of managers of personnel, you would find that there are many of them in every company. On the average, in all firms one of every twelve employees is a manager of personnel in the sense that he has reporting subordinates. This means that there are, on average, eight subordinates for every manager. Actually, in lower-level operations jobs, the ratio of supervised to supervisors is about twelve to one, and, among exempt-level jobs, that ratio is about three to one.

The essence of some of the critical problems of the traditional view as to who are the managers of personnel can be found in these statistics. There are too many managers of personnel for effective operations. Typically, managers have far too few subordinates to do the management of personnel job effectively.

New thinking with respect to organizational structuring will increase the average supervised-to-supervisory ratios. These organizational changes are required for more effective operation of the business, but they will also help to improve the effectiveness of managing personnel, because the result will be a broader "span of management." These organizational changes alone, however, will not be enough.

When there was largely a programmatic method of managing personnel, it was possible to have many managers and low supervisory ratios, although the system, in fact, probably did not work so well as we assumed at the time. But because the programs themselves managed, in the sense that they narrowly prescribed the latitude of managerial judgment, it probably was satisfactory not many years ago to designate each person who supervised the work of any number of people as the person with authority and responsibility for making personnel management decisions. A delegative style of managing personnel requires more know-how, experience, and skill to manage personnel effectively. Under these conditions, the old system of designating everybody who directed the work of others as their manager for purposes of personnel management will not work. This means that we will have to redefine just who the managers of personnel are and what they do.

THE MANAGERS

With respect to the management of personnel, we need to identify three types of management and therefore three categories of managers. Two of these now exist. Someone will probably find better labels, but until that time, we can identify these three types of managers of personnel as: executives, managers, and directors.

Executives: Naturally, executive managers of personnel do the most important things; but the greatest amount of their time is not necessarily spent managing people. The executive managers decide the personnel policy management issues; they approve requirements, including any required programs; they determine the systems of managing personnel; they approve and direct the establishment of appropriate guidelines and consultative practices; and they prescribe required auditing procedures. Executive managers also affect the management of personnel in such activities as strategic planning and deployment of assets throughout the firm.

As far as managing people is concerned, however, executives manage only those who report directly to them. They may, as a matter of choice, extend their management of personnel by the closeness with which they review personnel decisions. But if there is to be effective management of personnel at the top, executives must restrict the persons over whom they personally exercise managerial authority to those jobs and persons whom they know well.

Directors and Managers: Directors of personnel are all those who have subordinates. They see to it that required work is done; they are the operational managers at every level of the firm. They assign the work to be done and design jobs, with due consideration of the work to be done and the skills of those available to do the work. The directors train subordinates in how to do the work the best way, or they work with those subordinates to help *them* determine the most effective way to get work done. Directors use assigned personnel as well as the physical resources available at the time to accomplish the missions of their unit. The directors themselves perform work in most instances and therefore are part of the working group.

The directors are, in effect, all those who supervise work. They might be called supervisors. I like the word "directors" because it is a new term, more descriptive of what is really done and—deservedly, I think—has more status.

Identification of the directors would essentially involve a referencing of the existing company organization charts at a given point in time. The units established in organizational charting represent the units identified to get work done and accomplish missions. The head of each such unit is a director of work. As an example, the director of industrial engineering would be the director of industrial engineering people at that location. But he would not necessarily be the manager of personnel of industrial engineering people.

The difference would be that all who supervise the work of others are directors of that work, but many would not necessarily be managers of personnel; they would not be responsible for personnel management. All those who manage personnel would also be directing the work of some others.

Recognize that designation of managers of personnel from among directors of personnel is not a matter of level, rank, or salary grade. Designation of managers of personnel is based upon requirements for effective management as well as qualifications for the work and knowledge of jobs and people managed. Thus some very highly paid people would be directors of subordinates' work but not managers of personnel.

THE MANAGERS OF PERSONNEL

The managers of personnel are designated directors with the responsibility and the authority to make personnel decisions. They make personnel decisions with respect to persons in designated units. This would always be those in their own unit. It may often include employees in other units, each of which has a director.

Managers of personnel make decisions about who is selected for employment and who is to be promoted. They make performance evaluation judgments and are responsible for determining and implementing actions to improve performance. They make decisions about pay levels and pay increases. This is, of course, just a partial or an illustrative list. Make a complete list of the personnel responsibilities of those designated as managers of personnel in your own firm. Recognize that the list itself may vary somewhat at different levels of the organization or in different parts of the corporation.

Many who direct work cannot be expected to discharge such responsibilities. Many do not have the knowledge of personnel policies and practices or the skills of personnel that are necessary to discharge these responsibilities. The designation of managers of personnel from among the directors of personnel is thus an imperative in businesses today.

To carry out the responsibilities of the manager of personnel requires a considerable amount of personnel know-how and knowledge of your own firm's particular personnel programs, practices, and techniques. To acquire such knowledge requires considerable learning. Simply to sustain a satisfactory level of knowledge about personnel to carry out the responsibilities of the job of manager of personnel in a satisfactory manner requires at least one hundred hours of work each and every year. It simply does not make economic sense to expect such a time investment to acquire and sustain the level of personnel knowledge required if it is to be utilized for making decisions about only a few employees. It would be a very unproductive use of time, guaranteed to result in lower-than-attainable levels of productivity.

To make decisions about selection, training, pay, communications, et cetera also requires *skill*. For example, you cannot really be good at interviewing candidates for a position if you only do it a few times a year, even if your part in the selection input is limited. So much of personnel work is excellence in the application of personnel knowledge. To achieve and sustain that excellence requires practice; it involves doing it quite often. This means managing a significant number of people.

One other requirement for the effective management of personnel is to make sound judgments which can only come from experience and the precedents that many experiences provide. You need to have a lot of experience to be a good manager of personnel, and you will only have that experience if you practice this area of work for a considerable number of people.

There is, in other words, an appropriate "span of management" of personnel necessary in order to justify the level of knowledge of personnel required to do effective work and accumulate and sustain the required amount of skill and experience. There are no scientific formulas for what this "span of management" might be, but, as shown in *Exhibit 3-1*, it is a function of the level of the jobs (or the amount of technology involved in the jobs) and the diversity of jobs supervised. Considering these two variables, there may be as few as twenty people managed in terms of personnel or more than a hundred.

A company would probably average 50 to 150 directors of personnel per 1,000 employees *(Exhibit 3-2)*. Some of these directors of personnel would also be managers of personnel; many would not. You should expect between one of three and one of five directors also to be managers of personnel.

41

Exhibit 3-1

SPAN OF MANAGEMENT
Number of Employees Who Can Be Managed Effectively*

Level/Complexity of Jobs	Diversity of Jobs		
	Low	Medium	High
Low	100	70	40
Medium	70	40	30
High	40	30	20

*Refers to the management of personnel, not directors of work.

Exhibit 3-2

NUMBER OF DIRECTORS, MANAGERS,
AND PERSONNEL GENERALISTS

	Number per 1,000 Employees	
	Low (a)	High (b)
Directors	150	50
Managers	50	10
Personnel Managers	5	3

(a) Supervised-to-supervisory ratio about 7:1.
(b) Supervised-to-supervisory ratio about 20:1

These managers of personnel should be supported in their work by first-level personnel generalists. It is the role of the personnel generalist at all levels of the organization to support those managers who make personnel decisions. A personnel manager might support as few as three managers of personnel or as many as ten. There could, therefore, be as few as three first-level personnel managers per 1,000 employees in a company or as many as ten *(Exhibit 3-2)*.

All these guidelines and the restructuring to establish the job of manager of personnel are complicated by the nature of the operation, organizational structure, geographic locations, and size of facilities. But how well the organization is structured to *manage people well* is the critical issue considered here. In fact, the effective management of personnel should be a consideration in planning facilities, their location, and their size. Companies have more latitude in planning the size and location of facilities with information technology.

In fact, in some industries, personnel management considerations are a dominant factor in physical locations. A large retail chain, for example, will not locate in an area until it can build enough stores to achieve certain criteria of scale of operation. One of these is that there must be a sufficient sales volume to support an efficient warehouse. A second is that there must be a sufficient volume of business to justify local mass advertising. The third is that there must be a sufficient number of employees to support at least three managers of personnel and one personnel manager.

Of course, the manager of personnel need not be expert in the work that is being done. The director of personnel must be the expert, because it is the director who assigns work, trains, et cetera. On the other hand, the manager of personnel must be familiar with the work and the people and conversant with the technology of the work. The management of people is not a stand-alone skill that can be exercised independently of the work being done.

The directors of work would participate in personnel management decisions. They would, for example, give inputs to the manager of personnel. They know the details of the work, and they have insights about the people. This contribution of information by directors is critical to the effective management of personnel. However, decisions would not be "negotiated" or made on a consensus basis. Decisions are strictly the responsibility of the manager of personnel.

How the directors and the managers work together will likely vary a great deal. There are many specific relationships that will work well. Let each manager of personnel and the directors of personnel work this out together. Don't write a procedure or set a lot of rules. In every case, however, it is suggested that the decision-making authority must, in fact, remain with the manager of personnel, and the contribution of the director of work should only be informational.

This is not totally different from working relationships that have existed in management for many years. For example, plant foremen direct the work, but very often they only make recommendations with respect to critical personnel decisions. Foremen are frequently more leadmen than managers. It is the next level of factory management that, in fact, makes personnel management decisions with respect to the people who work in the various departments directed by the foremen. There are also precedents for these concepts in the limits on authority for expenditures that have been established in most business.

The directors remain the experts with respect to the work that must be done. The managers of personnel are the ones who are expert enough at the job of managing people. This does not involve the evolution of a new job but rather the assignment of an existing job only to those who can do the work well.

IMPLEMENTATION

The transition to the system of designating managers of personnel from among those who direct work is very difficult. Those who have undertaken such a change have found the intensity of feelings is sometimes extreme and the difficulties of bringing about change are very great. Fortunately, they have also found that results, in terms of increased effectiveness of the operation, are well worth the trouble and the trauma.

Every person who has one or more subordinates has been a

manager of personnel. When you implement these concepts, you are telling many of the people that they have less authority in matters of personnel. This obviously creates problems. Even though there isn't any facet of personnel from which directors would be excluded, their authority is diminished.

When the concept of the manager of personnel is implemented, you will hear many opposing arguments, reasons why it should not be done. Some may have substance, so all should be heard. However, many objections will simply reflect people's desire to keep what they have, thinking their new role is less, their status is diminished, and that they will lose power.

There isn't anything about the concept of the manager of personnel that is contradictory to the delegative management process. The goal of delegative management is to delegate personnel decisions into the organization to the level where there is knowledge of the jobs and of the people who do the work. However, it is also necessary that the delegation be to those who have the knowledge and the experience necessary to make these personnel decisions properly.

In spite of the need for and the logic in establishing managers of personnel throughout the organization, companies that have followed this course have found intense resistance. Keep in mind that some of these people who will no longer be managers of personnel but only directors of work will be quite high-level management persons. But those who became only directors have been just one source of resistance and resentment.

Some employees who are not directors of work may also have concerns about the implementation of the job of manager of personnel. Some employees will always be concerned about changes of any type. But some will also think (sometimes correctly) that they will be less favored under the new system than they were under the old system.

Some executives may see such a change as being disruptive to their operation, which it is. This type of change improves long-term results. But it is disruptive, and that may have a negative impact on short-term results.

Executives who preach the need for change are sometimes reluctant to go through the change and learn to manage in different ways. Perhaps above all else, there is a fondness on the part of executives with the notion that they can manage the business, every aspect of the business. There is comfort in the notion that they control everything and every person. It is tranquilizing to think that everything that is done reflects their own good judgment, judgment freqently embodied in some program or rule. Of course top executives are not really controlling operations now, at least not the management of personnel. The establishment of managers of personnel makes it clearer that executives do not control everyone.

For some who supervise people and who are not designated managers of personnel, the critical issue is loss of *authority* over others. This is the main cause of resistance to this change. To some degree, business may have to reap the results of years of glamorizing the "authority" of managing people. There is a need in some firms to reflect seriously on the whole concept of managerial authority.

In the only litigation we have ever been involved in, the attorney for the defense argued over and over again that the captain of a ship had complete and unchallenged authority. She used this argument in screening jurors and in cross-examining witnesses. We heard many times about the authority of a ship's captain. But that is not the way I learned it in the navy.

The navy emphasized the sacred responsibility of a ship's captain for the seaworthiness of the vessel and the safety of all those who sailed on her. It was only to fulfill those responsibilities that the captain was granted broad authority, and for no other reason. And there was no job in the navy monitored more closely than that of a ship's captain—to be certain that he fulfilled his responsibilities and did so with reasonable exercise of authority.

So it should be with managers. I think in business we have emphasized the authority of management too much. Officers and managers of public corporations do have legal authority, and that authority is very great. Managers must have the authority to manage. But authority is not an executive perk or an award. Authority must be granted only to run the business successfully.

The emphasis should be on the responsibility of management: to owners, to customers, the general public, and those who work in the firm—the "stakeholders" of the business. Authority over other people at work should be vested in managers only for the purpose of meeting responsibilities to the stakeholders. And the job of management, like that of a ship's captain, should be monitored carefully to be certain that the managers are discharging those responsibilities properly, with a reasonable exercise of power.

We probably never will define "leadership" to everyone's satisfaction. But I think one critical element of leadership is the effective discharge of responsibilities with minimal exercise of authority.

IT MUST BE DONE

It has always been said that management must manage. When a company designates managers of personnel, management still manages, but there are fewer managers, and the managers are better qualified to make personnel decisions.

When you look closely at organizations, the job of manager of personnel has existed to some degree anyway. In every company I know, there has been close review of the substantive personnel decisions of most supervisors. The real authority for making personnel decisions thus vests in fewer people than the table of organization indicates. But the trouble with this approach is that it is random. Too often the tight review vests decision making about people to those who really don't know the jobs or the people who do the jobs.

Each company, in fact, must find its own way toward some version of the delegative style of managing personnel, and each must move at its own pace. Some will see an opportunity and move quickly, gaining a competitive edge through more effective operations. Others will change, no doubt, only to the degree that circumstances force them to. When current systems break down totally and there are serious crises, then actions will be taken.

The critical actions involve the designation of the managers of personnel from among those who are now supervisors. Clearly, your criterion for selection should be the ability to make personnel decisions properly; factors such as rank, grade, or popularity are not relevant. The ability to manage personnel will, in turn, mean mostly evaluating who has done the job the best in the

47

past. Frequently, however, two or more directors will have demonstrated equivalent skill in personnel matters. Then selections must be made on predictive criteria and judgments about potential and proper career path. These selection criteria will be the primary basis for selecting first-time managers of personnel in the future.

There is much talk about "high-tech" in businesses. All businesses are higher-tech. Even the simplest, most traditional businesses have a greater diversity of positions and higher levels of technology in every area of their work. Test this proposition, in fact, by looking at your own firm ten years ago, and compare the number of technical positions and the level of technology then and now. Then extrapolate that change ten years into the future.

The simple and unarguable fact is that, with the levels of technology in almost all business today, personnel decisions must be made at the level where there is an understanding of the jobs. Also, with the increasing need for what has been called "high-touch" (and I think should be called "higher-touch"), personnel decisions must also be made at the level where the decision makers know the people. This requires far greater delegation of personnel decision making than has existed. But that delegation cannot be beyond the level of competency. This is why the delegative management style and the establishment of managers of personnel are an interrelated part of the evolution of a more effective system for managing people in the company.

The establishment of the managers of personnel is, therefore, an essential part of delegating personnel decisions into the organization sufficiently for effective operation. Along with evolving the appropriate sytem of delegative management and the designation of the managers of personnel, there is also, I think, the need to evolve a fundamentally different philosophy or attitude toward all who work in the firm and to review the role of those in the personnel department.

Chapter 4

EMPLOYEE PARTNERS

In addition to the basic matters of style in managing personnel and designating the managers of personnel, there are two other fundamental issues regarding the management of personnel. One involves the role and activities of the personnel department (chapter 5). The other is perhaps the most difficult and controversial matter: the basic attitude of those who run the firm regarding those who work in the firm. The attitude of the company toward those who work in the firm is a matter of philosophy and belief (what is *right*), as well as a practical business matter (what is effective).

THE PARTNERSHIP PHILOSOPHY

It is suggested that the basic attitude that companies increasingly must adopt, or work toward, is a "partnership philosophy." In its most simple form, a partnership philosophy is one that views every employee at every level of the organization as a working "partner" or "associate." It views each employee as performing a vital activity and recognizes that each employee has certain inherent authority in his work and that employees have basic rights as well as prescribed responsibilities.

Employee Partners as a Way of Managing Personnel: Under this philosophy, those who work in the firm are not partners in a legalistic sense; the word "partner" is meant in a business sense. A partner is one who works with others in the firm as an associate; they work together in a common endeavor.

Employee partners may perform the same duties as those cast in different roles. They may engage in the same activities as they would under some other view of the employees' role or status. The differences are not so much in what work people do, but how they do that work, as well as employees' perceptions of themselves and their company.

A partnership philosophy is highly egalitarian. The differences that exist between employees, or employee groups, are related to the nature of work which is done. Where differences in pay, benefits, or conditions of work exist at all, for example, they exist because of legal requirements; because different work necessitates different pay plans; or because of labor market needs.

Partners are individuals, each with his own skills and talents and each with his own ambitions and objectives. Partners must recognize the need to work effectively, and they must be self-motivated, partly because they work in an environment that promotes initiative. They work with others effectively because others are their partners, and each partner recognizes that the effectiveness of each person is important to the results achieved by all.

The partnership philosophy is not permissive. Partners at every level in the organization must adhere to policies and required rules. Where employees are viewed as partners, there are fewer rules, but those that exist have to be followed more closely. In essence, the very fact that there is greater latitude of action inherent in a partnership philosophy requires greater organizational discipline, but only with respect to essential matters that influence the effectiveness of work. Partners are expected to exercise self-discipline. Partners must respect essential rules, recognizing the need for structure and discipline, within which they have great latitude. Partners should respect the rulemakers because they are respected by the rulemakers.

There must be trust in a company that adopts the partnership philosophy. Employees at every level must have a high degree of trust in their peers, in those in higher-level positions and, equally, in those in lower-level positions. There must be a high degree of reliance on others to do their jobs and do them well. Each person must have confidence that all others are performing their responsibilities to the best of their abilities.

This high degree of trust reflects itself in basic attitudes. For instance, there must be an assumption that every person at every level has the same degree of trustworthiness, self-motivation, and responsibility as every other person. The president must assume, for instance, that the file clerk has just as much pride in his work and strives just as much for excellence as the president does.

There is a harsh side to the partnership philosophy. It necessarily places a considerable responsibility on individuals and requires certain types of personal qualities. For example, those who cannot accept authority or who are inclined to hold back and not do their best cannot work effectively in a partnership environment. Such people must be reassigned or, if no suitable assignment can be found where they will or can perform as a partner of the firm, they must then necessarily become one of the firm's alumni.

It is clear that the partnership philosophy is not practiced in most companies today. Some alternative is practiced, if not consciously adopted, at least in the way the company's personnel practices are applied and in the attitude toward employees which is reflected in daily actions and decisions.

The practice most firms follow, consciously or unconsciously, is simply that management is one group or class and that all others who work for the firm are "employees"; this is the traditional boss/worker relationship. It is perhaps the natural attitude of managers toward others in the firm and will automatically be reflected in the firm's views and actions in the absence of some soul-searching and the evolution of a company culture that reflects the partnership philosophy.

The view that those who work in the firm are "employees" is very traditional. It is a view inherited from an era when those who owned the business typically managed the business. Managers were owners, and employees were paid help. Today, managers are also paid employees of the company and not owners. The employees' view is also inherited from an era where work assignments were typically simple and routine, and those who directed the work knew every job and a great deal about the work that was done. Then the manager could be the boss. These conditions have changed; jobs are more complex and diverse. No manager knows all the jobs in the firm and cannot be expected to understand the technology of many of these jobs.

51

Perhaps most of all, the employees' view is inappropriate because all people who work in a firm are, to some extent, managers. In yesteryear, managers were those who had responsibility for assets or people, but today we must also manage knowledge. Today, with so much technology, more and more people determine their own work methods and therefore, in part, manage themselves.

Specific Needs for a Partnership Philosophy: There are basically two reasons why there is a need for a partnership philosophy. One is very practical: The partnership philosophy contributes to greater effectiveness of work. The broader view is that employees, who are a very large voting group, will be more inclined to be supportive of our free-choice enterprise system if they are treated like partners in the system.

There is no precise data yet regarding the relationship among basic attitudes or philosophies toward employees and productivity. Productivity studies that have been made suggest at least that more of a partnership philosophy is an integral part of increasing employee productivity. Almost all successful productivity improvement efforts have included some form of worker involvement. Also, the adoption of a more delegative method of managing personnel involves worker determination of better work methods. But people will respond more positively to involvement and delegation of authority when they are viewed more as partners than as paid employees.

A partnership philosophy also affects productivity because it has to do with the conditions under which people work, and it produces a climate that is more conducive to each person doing his best. When employees are partners, the company has created an environment where employees will more likely strive for excellence and they will tend to work more cooperatively toward a common goal, because they see themselves as part of the enterprise.

When a partnership environment is created, employees have a commitment to themselves and to their organization. It makes the difference between doing what one is told to do and doing what one knows needs to be done. It makes the difference between just obeying rules versus carrying out the work that must be done with commitment and initiative.

The effectiveness of people at work is determined by a number of variables. One is the talent that people have to do their work. Another is the method by which the work is done. Last is the attitude of the people and their inclination to do their best. The partnership philosophy has little to do with the talent people bring to work. The company's attitude toward employees does impact methods and procedures by which work is done, largely because employees themselves contribute to more effective methods of work. The attitude toward people is probably the most important single factor determining the inclination to do one's best.

The broader issues of political attitudes are difficult to deal with, but they are quite important in the long run. One of the basic problems facing all businesses today is that they operate in a political environment that is generally unfavorable and frequently hostile. There has been a parade of laws that have made the operation of a business more difficult. Yet the business community has within its walls the largest single voting constituency. Those who work for business enterprises, those who have retired from business, and those dependent on people who work for businesses represent well over one-half of all eligible voters.

How is it possible for laws and regulations to be passed which harm the business when the business community has potentially such a large voting block? The answer is most likely that those who work in the business do not feel that they are a part of the business. If employees really felt that they were a part of the business system, they would be inclined to view differently the laws and regulations affecting the system and to make their views known to those who pass the laws.

No one firm's personnel philosophy will change the voting inclination of working men and women. However, if many working people felt more a part of the business system and if they perceived a clear relationship between the vitality of the business system and their own well-being, then the political balance might change. The result would probably be continued social progress, but in a manner supportive of a sound and viable enterprise system. The result would lead to relatively more political concern for the workers as contrasted to the nonworker.

Creating a Partnership Environment: For the company that

sees merit in thinking through and perhaps changing its basic attitude toward those who work in the firm, the questions are then what should it do and how should it proceed. Companies should think in terms of evolutionary change. A personnel philosophy or environment will not result because some policy pronouncement is made. This matter involves consideration of basic changes in the way work is done, the way business is conducted and the attitudes of people throughout the organization. It is necessary, therefore, to think in terms of a change process which may take a number of years.

The company needs to consider first its style of management. A partnership philosophy cannot exist, for instance, where there is a bureaucratic organization. The system of management most conducive to a partnership philosophy is that described as "delegative management." This managerial style gives the individual the right and the responsibility to develop those methods, practices, procedures, and activities that optimize his effectiveness.

A company must also examine carefully the environment that the company creates with its rules, regulations, and practices. Many of the rules and requirements, particularly for operations people, which have been evolved to meet some specific need or objective, create an environment that is the exact antithesis of the partnership environment. There are so many rules and regulations that apply only to operations people that this fact in itself creates a "them-and-us" environment. A company needs, therefore, to examine very carefully the environment it creates and remove or modify all rules and regulations that would impede or preclude the evolution of a partnership environment.

To create a partnership philosophy, a firm should, therefore, first examine the work environment it has created. Then the company should consider some affirmative actions. There are many possibilities, but four that have worked provide, perhaps, the best starting place. These are: having employees' views determinative in certain matters, including measure of employee success in the firm's information system, having at least one board member with considerable knowledge of personnel, and developing some form of compensation that particularly benefits non-managers.

54

THE ENVIRONMENT WE HAVE CREATED

The environment that most firms have created does not reflect the partnership philosophy. Too often, inefficiencies and low levels of productivity are blamed on pressure from unions, the government, and external conditions. But some elements of the environment of work that the company creates also contribute to negative attitudes and low productivity.

All companies have classes of employees. Each of these classes tends to have its own status or special benefits or privileges or all of these. To many people, the classes often appear to be artificial; to those in the less privileged classes, they seem discriminatory.

Many firms, for instance, have exempt versus nonexempt classes. On the surface, these are established to meet legal requirements. But a company can meet legal requirements in the way it pays people without setting classes which relate to legal definitions rather than any substantive conditions of the jobs involved or the operations of the business.

Other firms make class distinctions between direct and indirect workers. There was a time when this distinction was important in bookkeeping and cost accounting, but, with advanced accounting systems and utilization of computers, there is little business need for such distinctions today, and they serve only the purposes of status and privilege.

In most companies, some employees are paid a wage while others are paid a salary. If those paid a wage work forty hours, they get paid for forty hours. If they miss a day or an hour, they do not get paid for that time. Others in the firm are paid a salary and are better off. They, at least, have some excused time, such as sick days for which they are paid even if they do not work. Other salaried employees, such as executives, do not get docked at all if they miss an hour or a day or a week.

Most employees have prescribed vacation periods, and frequently the time when they may take their vacations is set by the company. The same is true with respect to holidays. Other employees, however, have much broader latitude as to time off. They may take vacations they think are appropriate and when they want the time off. Those with extra privileges may work just as many days or even more, but they are treated differently and in a more favored manner.

For many people, not only are their jobs assigned, but the way they do their work is strictly regulated. They may not perform their duties differently from the prescribed manner. If they do, they get bad marks, even if the results are better. But nobody tells other employees how to do their jobs. Professional people as well as executives typically find their own "right way" to work. They have latitude to do their jobs in the way they find to be most effective.

Some employees punch time clocks or fill out time sheets while others don't. The majority of employees have established lunch hours and rest periods. Others take their lunch and rest breaks when they need them or when they choose. Some employees have set starting times and stopping times. Others decide for themselves when to come to work and when to leave. These are also examples of practices common in most firms which create an environment where some employees are treated more favorably than others.

Obviously, some rules are necessary in order to conduct the affairs of the business in an orderly manner. In a manufacturing plant, for example, when the machines start up, all production employees must be there to do their jobs. When the machines shut down, there is no point in their staying any longer. In all cases where the work of one employee is dependent upon other employees, all must be there at the same time. Starting and finishing times, however, are very broadly applied in operations-level jobs where there are no compelling reasons why all employees should be at work at the same time.

The issue is not, however, whether *necessary* rules and regulations are appropriate. The issue is whether any such rules, classes, or benefits should be applied unless they are required by the nature of the work or contribute to more effective operations. The fact of the matter is that many practices that are applied in business exist because high-level executives believe that lower-level persons will not do the "right thing" unless there are rules that tell them what they must do.

There is the concern, for example, that, unless the company

restricts the number of sick days people are allowed, employees would take time off and claim to be sick when indeed they were not; that, unless there were starting and stopping times, people would not work a reasonable number of hours and get the jobs done that are assigned to them; and that, unless there were penalties for lateness, people would be late.

Such rules and regulations, however, tell some employees that they are different, and the differences are not pleasant for them to hear. The employer is telling some employees that, without these rules, they would not do their best; they would cheat, and they would malinger. But the fact that these rules and regulations do not apply to all persons carries still another message. Companies are telling their people, for instance, that executives can be counted on to work hard while others can not. The rules imply that some employees, such as executives, can be counted on to do their best whereas others will do less than their best unless they are made to do their best. Rules and regulations tell people that some employees take pride in their work but that others will tend to do shoddy work unless they are monitored very carefully.

The truth of the matter is that there are many in the managerial ranks who genuinely believe that they and their peers are responsible, hard-working, honest, dependable, trustworthy, and proud of their work, and that lower-level employees are not. Many rules and regulations are put into effect because of this belief. They are put into effect because the rulemakers believe that they will always do the right thing and others will seldom, if ever, do the right thing unless compelled to do so. To respond to such an attitude we must always ask, "At what level of the organization do people become irresponsible?"

In all of this, there is an interesting assumption: that highly paid people have certain qualities that are lacking in people who are paid less. There is, however, no evidence that there is a relationship between the amount a person is paid and his pride in his work, his job level and his desire to do his best, or his salary grade and his integrity.

To some extent, the very rules and regulations, and the thinking that they express, may represent a self-fulfilling prophecy. If you tell people often enough that they do not take pride in their work, sooner or later they will stop taking pride in their work. If you keep telling people, by the way you behave as well as by what you say, that they cannot be trusted, they may well become less trustworthy. If, in the way people are required to work, it is made clear to them that those in authority do not consider them either competent or responsible, there will be a tendency for them to become less competent and less responsible.

No single rule creates an environment that contributes to this malaise and quite likely causes lower productivity. As a practical matter, even a considerable collection of rules—if they are properly applied and clearly explained—does not create the environment of a regulated work place. But when rules are plainly established for the purpose of preventing people from doing poor work or behaving badly, then the implication is that they would be inclined to do poor work or cheat without the rules. Management is also saying to others, "We are superior," which necessarily implies that others are inferior.

Rules and regulations can also inhibit progress in some instances. If some person in an organization has an idea about how things can be done better, or if there are new circumstances that require some new action contrary to established rules, then there is a disinclination to proceed even when it is clearly the right thing to do. The rules themselves may have to be changed before individuals or units can proceed in the most effective manner. But changing rules takes time and effort and sometimes gets people in trouble.

One final difficulty with rules and regulations which are not clearly required is that they may become the purpose rather than a means to an end. Rules are there for a purpose, supposedly to contribute to the effectiveness of work and the welfare of the business, but the presence of rules tends to become the preoccupation. People are motivated to follow the rules rather than to work effectively.

MANAGEMENT ACTIONS

Companies can provide a partnership philosophy and deregulate the work environment in a number of ways. One involves top-management actions. Ideally, each such action should have a double merit: it should be of value in its own right, and it should contribute to a partnership philosophy.

In some personnel decisions, there may be alternatives with approximately equal costs and advantages to the company. In these cases, it is suggested as a matter of management practice that employees' views be *determinative*. The alternate answers might have equivalency to management, but some of these alternatives may be far more preferable to employees than others. In such cases, employees should be given an opportunity to express their preferences. Their preferences should be the factor which most determines final management decisions; employees' views should be determinative.

Employees should know when their views are determinative. There may not be many cases where the employees' views are determinative, but even a few cases each year can be an important part of making employees aware of the fact that they are part of the process; they are "partners" of the firm.

If a firm determines that its benefits package needs to be improved, which particular benefit is improved is usually not of great importance to the company. This is one instance where employees' views should be determinative. When there is a cutback in work, companies should consider giving employees a choice between reduction in force and spreading work among all employees. In high-tech businesses, matters determined by employees may even involve work methods, because how employees prefer to do the work can affect how well the work is done.

There are many ways in which companies could get employees' views on such matters. Properly structured, focus attitude studies would be one. With today's technology, as a matter of fact, companies could get employees' views on a specific matter within twenty-four hours with telephone votes.

A second management action would involve business measures of personal success. Part of the measures of the success of the firm would then be measures of employee success. Such an action recognizes employees as partners, whose welfare and success are one of the basic goals of the enterprise.

With the emergence of computerized human resources information systems, companies measure the success of the enterprise in terms of some employee data as well as other business statistics. What is suggested is that companies also measure how successful the business is in satisfying the reasonable goals of its people.

There are a number of such measures of personnel success which may be a part of the business measurement system. They would include:

- Employee pay progress: for each employee, by groups of employees, and for employees overall.

- Job security measures: including terminations as well as layoffs.

- Job career progress: for individuals and groups, how many employees benefited from promotions and how these numbers compared with outside hires.

- Health and safety measures: work-related illnesses and accidents.

- Growth in knowledge and experience: not only for purposes of succession planning, but to see the degree to which employees are growing in their work life.

- Measures of employee confidence and job satisfaction.

Such measures have some business value in that they are proxy attitude surveys. But it also seems right that a company measures its success at least in part by how well those who create the wealth are achieving personal success. Certainly, the implications to the employees are not only that the company cares, but that it considers those who work in the firm as important stakeholders.

I have also urged companies, for a very long time, to have at least one member of the board of directors who has special personnel knowledge, training, and background. I have done this because I thought it would be a sound management practice and that it was critical to the board in discharging some of its responsibilities.

Every member of the board must first and foremost be fully qualified to fulfill the legal and fiduciary responsibilities of the board, and each director must be a contributor to the general duties and activities of the board. Only from among generally qualified people should those with special expertise, knowledge, and skills be sought. This rule applies equally to the director who has special personnel qualifications.

The director with personnel knowledge would not be an advocate or an ombudsman. The role would not be to defend employees or to be their representative. Rather, the person with special personnel knowledge would bring employee considerations to bear in basic policy and strategic decisions which are made at the board level. He would also have first-hand knowledge in helping his colleagues on the board review the appropriateness of personnel actions and thinking, which should be an important part of the board's responsibilities.

This person with special personnel know-how would obviously have great value in the board's discharge of its responsibilities in executive selection and executive compensation. But he would also have special value in reviewing compensation plans which affect all employees, such as pension plans. Directors must increasingly also explore, discuss and review matters such as compliance with government regulations, succession throughout the organization, and the general employee relations climate of the firm.

The board member with personnel know-how and experience would thus have many specific values. That member would also be able to reflect the views and thinking of employees throughout the firm. This should help the board make sound decisions. Because employees know this, and they know the board thinks their views are important, they would likely feel more like partners in the firm.

Another management matter which companies might consider is to establish one important form of compensation which is of special benefit and value to nonmanagement workers. Companies have many special pay plans and benefits for executives. Some of these meet the special needs of that particular group of employees. But all other employees have special needs also; such as the need to build an estate for various purposes, like the edu-

61

cation of their chidren. It would do a great deal toward creating more positive attitudes if there were some special compensation program to deal with their particular needs. It would also add a financial element toward reenforcing an employee/partner view toward those who work in the firm.

My favorite would be the establishment of an employee-class stock. This would be a second-class stock; like a Class B stock. However the employee-class stock would only be traded between employees and the company. The company would sell the stock to employees for cash or distribute it as part of a profit-sharing plan. The price would be geared to the book value of the company. When the employee leaves the company for any reason, he would sell the stock back to the company at the then book value.

During the period of ownership, "bonuses" would be paid to employees for each share of employee-class stock owned. These payments would simulate dividends. Because it would be a pre-tax item, the amount of the "bonus" could be twice that of the ordinary stock dividend. In this way, the employees would have a very favorable investment vehicle; with the yield in most companies greater than the most secure investments; with growth potential geared to the profits of the business; and a high level of security, because the stock could only decline in value if the company lost money.

SPECIFIC PRACTICES

Another way to deregulate the work environment and move toward a partnership environment involves changing personnel practices. In some of what has been covered, there have been inherently specific suggestions for actions which might reinforce an employee/partner relationship in a company. Here is a checklist of ten items. Your personnel professionals can think of others. If they need help, have them ask the employees themselves.

• Eliminate hourly status for any employee.

• Post all job openings, including management openings.

- Establish flex-time work hours.

- Make certain that all benefits are equivalent for all who work in the firm.

- Establish an effective system everywhere in the company where questions and complaints will be heard and dealt with reasonably and equitably.

- Be sure that there is an equitable basis for layoffs; make that item a matter of employee determination.

- Eliminate every rule unless it has a clear and compelling business purpose.

- Assure adequate recognition of achievement, not only through higher pay but through personal commendations in company communications.

- Provide special training and education for those who are having difficulty doing their jobs effectively; and when that doesn't work, provide outplacement for unsatisfactory performers.

- Have a quick-response communications system; and tell employees important things about the company even when it's bad news.

PRECEDENTS AND CASES

For those who may think that the partnership philosophy is idealistic, I would refer them to the specific action steps just outlined and ask, "Why not?" To achieve everything suggested, particularly in a brief period of time, is perhaps unrealistic and idealistic. But there is, I think, ample evidence to suggest that in today's work environment some steps and some movement in the directions outlined are vital to an effective work force.

You might also ask if it has even been done. There are elements of this partnership philosophy in the personnel practices of such outstanding firms as IBM, Eastman Kodak, and J.C. Penney. I can tell you of one case where this approach toward those who work in the firm was implemented in the extreme. It was my own company.

Mine was a small company; we only had about 50 employees. It was a professional business, and we operated in the suburbs. These were, no doubt, ideal conditions which facilitated a partnership environment. But it is a case for reference anyway, and at least I practiced what I preach.

Our office was open from 9:00 to 5:00, five days a week. But there were no starting times or quitting times for any employee. Those who answered the phones, for example, knew when they had to be at the office to answer the phones. They were there or they arranged for someone else to take their place.

In terms of amount of work, we had a 35–150–2000 hour guideline. This meant that our standard was a 35-hour week; that we should all work an average of 150 hours a month; and no one should work more than 2000 hours a year, including overtime.

We had no exempt or nonexempt status. We had a profit-sharing bonus plan which applied equivalently to every person. Those who had to receive overtime pay, by law, had such payments deducted from their bonuses.

All employees received the same benefits. There were no scheduled vacations or holidays. People took the holidays they wanted to take, consistent with the need to get the work done. They did the same with vacations. We had no sick days or sickness insurance. If people got sick they got paid. Their salaries continued until they were well.

Each of our office personnel had assigned areas of work. For example, I had a secretary (we called them consulting associates because that was more decriptive of what they really did) whose main job was to support me in my work. There was typing to be done. I would always give my tapes to my associate, and she handed back the completed work. But I never asked who actually did the typing. Our office personnel worked out their own work methods. They knew what needed to be done and how to do it best. I have never seen a more effective or committed group of workers. It can be done.

IDEALISM OR A PRACTICAL BUSINESS OBJECTIVE?

I have held these basic views for many years. My thinking process started when I was Personnel Manager of Schick, Inc., in Lancaster, Pennsylvania. In that job I got to know thousands of working people very well.

For many years I have urged these views on client companies, but with little success. Perhaps my failure was due to my own inadequacies. But I think the lack of interest was also due to the fact that for many years my arguments were based largely on what seemed *right*, and on a very great faith in the initiative, willingness to work, and responsibility of American working men and women.

The employee-partner view also seemed to be consistent with our national heritage. It seemed to be a style which built on the character and traditions of American workers.

All that thinking is unproven and does sound idealistic. To some in personnel, the employee-partner view seemed out of step with programmatic personnel practices. The philosophy was contrary to the trend toward bigger and more bureaucratic practices in business and government alike. Some top executives dismissed this thinking abruptly and thought I was crazy.

There have been enough cases and precedents by now to prove, I think, that an employee-partner view is right and effective. With the increase in technology, a movement toward such an attitude concerning those who work in the firm is essential.

I am not urging the ideal business society or some form of utopia at work. I do urge a change of attitude by executives toward those who work in the firm and the implementation of some specific practices which will promote an employee-partner environment. We simply must end the "them and us" atmosphere to achieve the turnaround in employee productivity that is so essential to the success of many firms and the economic revitalization of our country.

Chapter 5

THE PERSONNEL DEPARTMENT

It was more than a dozen years ago that a business friend made the important distinction between the management of personnel and personnel management. Management has to do with recruiting required talent and the correct deployment of that talent; the many decisions and actions involving the appraisal, organization, communication, pay, training; and all other facets of managing personnel. Personnel management, by contrast, is what people in the personnel department do. This involves work to support those who manage personnel. So, what those who are in the personnel department do, and how well they perform this work, is a critical and integral part of the management of personnel.

THE EVOLUTION OF THE PERSONNEL ORGANIZATION

Personnel department activities have gone through a number of distinct phases before reaching their current status and role. It is not unusual for any function in business to go through evolutionary phases. For the personnel area, these distinct phases are of historical interest in order to understand the field, to judge the state of development of the personnel department in each firm, to develop people suitable to carry out the current responsibilities of the personnel department, to prepare for possible future activities, and to evaluate the contribution of the personnel organization. Personnel activities emerged shortly after World War I. Those who were in personnel work at that time had two responsibilities: selecting employees and keeping labor unions out of the business.

They practiced what, by today's standards, was a crude employment technique known as "gate hiring." Job selection depended on one person's first-hand knowledge of those who lived in the same community or perhaps had worked for the firm before. In keeping unions out, the personnel representative carried out his activities in whatever way he thought best. Those who first filled what can now be recognized as personnel jobs were typically ex-plant foremen or former industrial engineers. They had no knowledge or experience in "personnel"; there wasn't any. This was the first phase in the evolution of the personnel function.

The second phase in the evolution of the personnel department started in the 1930s with the passage of such legislation as The National Labor Relations Act, The Social Security Act, and The Fair Labor Standards Act. The National Labor Relations Act fostered unionization and created the need for bargaining knowledge and skills. The Fair Labor Standards Act created the need for the first basic elements of wage and salary administration. Social Security laws and union pressure for retirement plans required development of experience in employee benefits.

In the second phase, the personnel function essentially experienced two dramatic changes. For one thing, the function took on a number of new activities, many of which were essentially administrative or service-oriented. These included management of the parking lot and the cafeteria, maintenance of employee records, and frequently the publication of company newsletters for employees. The personnel function also evolved some new technologies which were unique to the personnel function and of considerable importance to management. It was these technological changes that really brought about a new type of personnel activity and a new type of personnel person.

For instance, job evaluation plans were instituted. Employment testing as a mangement tool also emerged during this period. Training of operations-level employees was developed to a very fine art during this period. Information gathering in a formal way also emerged in phase two of the evolution of the personnel function.

During this period, those in key personnel positions came from various backgrounds. There was, however, a new breed of personnel people who applied the new personnel technologies and practices and who viewed personnel work as a career. There was need for both technical competency and a facility for establishing relationships with others in management. Many in personnel became highly competent and highly skilled in their fields, and their abilities and efforts were the basis for the continuing evolution of the personnel function.

The third phase in the evolution of the personnel function was characterized by the development of a full-service staff organization. Personnel departments in the third phase grew to be large organizations, requiring skills in managing their own group.

During this third phase, personnel people started assuming important elements of line authority. For instance, labor relations people negotiated contracts. They had limits of authority, as is true of many management activities. The latitude of the labor relations manager is broader than that of some managers and less than others, but it is considerable.

Similarly, the authority of the personnel department in selection and screening became quite substantial. Of course, line managers usually still made final employment decisions. They chose from among a very limited group of candidates; candidates who had been selected by personnel people. Therefore, to a large degree, it became the employment people in the personnel department who made critical decisions affecting people brought into the organization.

In the third phase of the personnel function, the personnel department assumed new roles. Personnel people investigated people problems. For instance, when companies experienced excessive turnover, members of the personnel department were called upon to look into the problem and come up with specific recommendations for a solution. In this phase, personnel departments also spent a significant amount of time on practical research activities. Companies increasingly expected people in the personnel department to keep abreast of the field and to know when new practices and techniques evolved.

During this third phase, the personnel field developed truly unique knowledge and experience which was usable throughout the firm and not possessed by those in other functions. Some of this information and knowledge consisted of rather sophisticated personnel subjects. Personnel people in this third phase needed lay knowledge in a number of academic disciplines, such as law, psychology, economics, mathematics, and sociology. Personnel people also had to learn how to utilize all this knowledge in a practical way to benefit the firm and support management in increasing the effectiveness of those who worked in the organization.

Most of all, in the third phase personnel people developed new programs and practices. These were developed in every facet of personnel. It was the main activity of people in the personnel department; the basis for the programmatic system for managing personnel previously decribed.

Increasingly, those who worked in the personnel field did so because they chose this line of work as a career. Many of those who worked in the field had been educated in personnel work and had a considerable amount of diversity and experience in the field. In varying degrees, the function had become an accepted and respected part of the organization.

Phase four started to emerge in some leadership companies in the early 1970s. This fourth phase is not basically characterized by any additional areas of activity. There are no new departments, and no new knowledge areas have been added. Essentially, the knowledge and skill required to carry out the basic personnel mission increased only as business itself grew more complex, as new laws emerged, and as contemporary social values continued to change. The characteristics which distinguish personnel in the fourth phase as contrasted to the third phase are the role of the personnel group, the resulting expectations of personnel people, and the standards of performance which management sets for them. In the fourth phase the personnel department has become an integral part of the management process.

In the fourth phase it is not sufficient for personnel to be a full-service organization that is available to management. Personnel is a part of management and must take an active rather than a passive or reactive role. Those in personnel not only respond to problems but develop affirmative programs which are a necessary part of the plans and activities of management. Personnel is no longer an organization apart from operations but is itself a part of the business system.

The technical excellence of personnel must be maintained, but even excellence in the knowledge of personnel is insufficient in the mature personnel organization. The special knowledge of personnel people must be to relate personnel work effectively to the operations of the enterprise. Actions must be geared to the operational and strategic plans of the firm. Personnel actions must visibly make positive contributions to the achievement of the objectives of the enterprise.

The mature personnel organization is more than a collection of functional departments, such as compensation and employment. These departments may still exist, but their work is so interrelated that they are working as a project group in personnel matters rather than as separate entities. Each function in personnel must recognize that each area has an impact on every other area and that everything done in one area of personnel affects every other area of personnel.

To understand the nature of personnel organizations in this fourth phase, it is helpful to illustrate things that are done now that were not done or done infrequently and to a limited extent in the third phase of the evolution of the personnel function. Here are some examples.

- Personnel people demonstrate skills in helping line managers make more effective people decisions.

- Key people recognize that their area is people at work, but not in an abstract sense. Their area of work is people at work in *their* business, and their effort is a business effort focusing attention on utilization of the human talents within their organization.

- There is a demonstrated ability to relate personnel activities, decisions, and plans to the business and its objectives.

- There is a concern and demonstrated activity, even in the absence of a corporate commitment, to increase productivity through more effective personnel management and to structure and administer personnel programs so that increased productivity is at least a by-product of personnel activities.

- There is work toward the development of more usable data and information guidelines so that personnel decisions are made in a more objective manner with some quantifiable basis.

- There is some focusing of the personnel department's organization on its "customers": the corporate group, the divisions, and the sections and locations of the firm.

- Personnel people understand the needs and aspirations of working people and factor these elements into the management processes.

- Such organizations have learned to leverage personnel knowledge to operating units. They translate their technology and their language into usable forms which can be applied by line people who must make people decisions and deal with working people throughout the company.

- Work in the mature personnel organization is invariably systems work. Each functional section of the personnel organization interacts well and effectively with others.

Somewhat more than one of every 100 people who work in business now do personnel work; they work in the personnel department. There are about one million people doing personnel work now. More than 90 percent of all those who have ever done personnel work are actively doing that work now.

More than half of all the work done by those in the personnel department is required work; work which must be done because the firm is in business; e.g., compliance with government laws and regulations. This means that less than half the time available in the personnel department is contributive; in the sense that the time is directed at solving problems, gathering useful information, or working on new and more effective personnel practices. Therefore, the firm with a personnel ratio of .5 or less is allocating no time at all for such contributive work.

71

BASIC ORGANIZATION OF THE PERSONNEL DEPARTMENT

In connection with the developmental project on the effective management of the personnel organization, a general model for organizing the personnel department has been evolved as an analytic tool *(Exhibit 5-1)*.

There is, of course, the top personnel officer or more than one person in the office of the chief personnel officer. A second job involves all first-level personnel management jobs throughout the organization. This is the personnel generalist at every level of the company. Many have concluded that these jobs are the most important personnel jobs in the company, aside from the job of the chief personnel officer.

Frequently, however, particularly in large corporations, there is a necessary intermediate level of personnel generalist. This may be simply because there are so many first-level personnel generalists. More often, it is also influenced by the fact that in

Exhibit 5-1

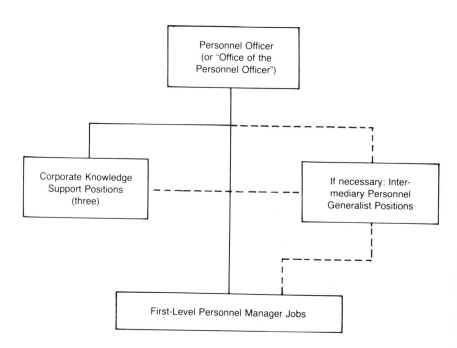

large companies there are multiple businesses, each headed by a senior general management executive with his own staff. One of the members of that staff should appropriately be a personnel generalist. While these intermediate personnel generalists may be an organizational necessity, they are also redundant in many ways. Never should they result in a barrier of information or relationships between the head personnel officer and first-level personnel management people.

Role, Function, and Objectives of the Chief Personnel Officer: During the past eight years I have had an opportunity to discuss their own positions with a number of senior personnel executives. The answer in each case was obviously different, but some general guidelines emerged from these discussions which might be helpful.

Above all else, the chief personnel officer is the personal personnel administrator for senior general management executives. In carrying out this activity, the chief personnel officer frequently becomes involved in very detailed and relatively low-level matters. But they are important activities because they serve senior general management executives. These chores must be done personally by the chief personnel officer. Performing well the job of personnel administrator for senior executives is the first and most important job of the chief personnel officer. Such work must always have the first priority and get immediate attention.

The chief personnel officer is also the chief personnel spokesman for the company. He speaks for management on critical issues. Therefore, it is a heavy responsibility; it is a role of high trust. In essence, the chief personnel officer must be able to answer questions of great substance as the chief executive officer would answer them.

The chief personnel officer is also the chief problem solver. It is the chief personnel officer who has to deal personally with the major problems. Because they are major problems, the chief personnel officer can never make a mistake in a project which he personally undertakes. Therefore, make certain that in carrying out this role you get the best support work possible; from inside or outside the company.

The chief personnel officer is also a source of knowledge.

He provides the basic personnel inputs which general management executives and the board use in their decision making. It is also very helpful to provide knowledge which may not have direct relevance to executive decisions, but which is useful and usable by senior executives in their relations with other senior executives, important outside people, and members of the board of directors.

Because personnel departments have grown substantially in size, the chief personnel officer is also an important manager of a large department, with a big budget. He is the knowledge chief and the personal leader of people in the personnel organization; whether they report to him by line, dashes, dots, or asterisks. He must see to their professional development and monitor their career progress.

First-Level Personnel Management: First levels of operating managers have always been viewed as the key to the excellence of the management of operations employees. Yet how can they manage with excellence without the support of knowledgeable and experienced first-level personnel people? In fact, don't the first- and second-level managers of personnel need *more* support (though perhaps a different type) than higher-level managers who are more experienced?

To have inadequate capability in the first levels of the personnel department may be the most critical weakness in the effective management of people. The best conceived and designed personnel programs and practices won't be effective unless they are applied well; and the implementation is done by the managers of personnel, *supported by first-level personnel generalists.*

In very general terms, while the corporate personnel organization determines what is to be done, it is the first-level personnel people who do it. While higher-level people in the personnel department focus on how we should improve personnel activities, the focus of the first levels of the personnel department is on how well we do what we are doing now. At the top, much of the thinking and focus of the work is on next month, next year, and even further in the future. At the first levels of the personnel organization, the focus is on today and tomorrow.

The top levels of personnel deal with broad concepts, with plans and strategies, and with considerations of employee relations overall; and thus tend to deal with employees as a group. The first levels of the personnel department deal with grass-roots issues—they are engaged in a series of "fire drills," and they spend most of their time dealing with *individuals*. It is at this first level *alone* where the individual employee is considered, and each of these individuals knows it.

In implementing personnel programs, the first-level personnel people are, to some extent, determining the real nature of the company's personnel programs. This process is similar to the fact that the government and the legislatures pass the laws, but the decisions of the courts and the regulations of government agencies affect what the laws really mean. Actually, first-level personnel people have more latitude in determining what policies and programs really mean than corporate people like to think or even believe. You can really only understand how this happens if you have worked at operations levels.

You may think, for example, that you have a certain performance appraisal system because the corporate office designed the form and set the procedures. And sure enough, people fill out the form in the manner prescribed and according to the schedule—usually. But we know from too many cases that there may be no performance appraisal at all in the operations; rather, a chore is carried out to meet a corporate requirement. What's more, you can't have high-quality performance appraisal unless there are qualified personnel people in the organization where the appraisals are made.

Intermediate Positions: Personnel generalists at large locations, at the division level, and at the group level have widely different duties. These jobs represent an example of how a job title or a job description may tell little about the job which is really done. They are, however, all intermediate, between the head of corporate personnel and the first-level personnel generalist. What they cannot or should not do is dilute the work done by the head of personnel or the first-level personnel generalists.

In a diversified business where different business areas have great latitude and the corporation has a delegative style of managing people, the personnel generalist at the business-area level has a job quite similar to a corporate personnel director. In a business characterized by one dominant business area, centralized decision making, and a programmatic style of managing personnel, all intermediate personnel generalists are largely representatives of the corporate personnel office and perform essentially administrative and monitoring activities.

Generally I urge the following with respect to the intermediate personnel generalist positions.

- Where there is a highly autonomous business area, view that business area's personnel head and his support staff as you would a separate company. It is essential that these business-area personnel directors should be active participants in developing corporate personnel policies, requirements, guidelines, and support work.

- Except for the autonomous business areas, have as few personnel generalists as possible between the head of corporate personnel and the first-level personnel generalist. All such intermediary positions should exist primarily to support high-level managers of personnel, just as first-level personnel generalists support managers of personnel throughout the organization. All other activities of these intermediate personnel generalists should be reviewed carefully and kept to a minimum.

- At the location level, allow personnel people other than the location personnel manager to do only *required* local personnel work; e.g., local hiring, local pay surveys, et cetera.

- Rarely should a division personnel manager or group personnel manager have any staff at all, except personal assistance to help him do his job.

Companies must now contain the growth and the number of people working in the personnel department. One place to do this is in these intermediate-level personnel generalist jobs. Another is with respect to corporate personnel staff specialists.

Corporate Personnel Support Staff: Control very tightly the number of people reporting to each corporate staff support person.

It is in these corporate personnel departments where the size of the personnel organization is most likely to become bloated. Avoid overspecialization on the part of the work of people filling such jobs. Also avoid compartmentalization; e.g., a person in the benefits department does only benefits work.

There is still a need for corporate knowledge support positions. However, the nature of these positions needs to be examined. Some companies that have made such a review have changed from the traditional functional breakdown: compensation, benefits, labor relations, training, communications, et cetera. They have tended to establish three types of knowledge support jobs.

The first of these is the information manager. This job includes compensation administration, benefits, and human resources information systems. The second is the manpower manager. This includes recruiting, organization, training and development, communications, and manpower controls. Finally, there is the relations manager. This individual handles union relations, EEO and other government regulatory matters, and external relations. There may also be an administration specialist.

INCREASING THE EFFECTIVENESS OF THE PERSONNEL DEPARTMENT

In the last two "personnel priorities" questionnaires distributed every other year to subscribers to *The Sibson Report*, "increasing the effectiveness of the personnel department" was among the top ten priority items. Follow-up showed the reason for this emphasis was simply that the personnel department had more and more tasks to do but, as a matter of cost containment, top management had put constraints on further growth in the relative size of the personnel department. Outlined here are some suggestions that came out of work for many firms on increasing the effectiveness of their personnel organizations. Some of these suggestions might be helpful in increasing the effectiveness of your own personnel department.

Perhaps most important, it is suggested that every proposed personnel activity or project should be evaluated by three criteria.

Only if the project gets high marks on each of the three should it be undertaken. The three criteria are:

- There must be some clear and apparent need or opportunity for the activity.

- There must be some clear relationship between the action which is contemplated and the result desired.

- The cost/value relationship must be clear and highly favorable.

Needs are not always obvious in personnel work, and opportunities are rarely provable. But the first of the three criteria for evaluating personnel projects says that there must be a clear and demonstrable need or opportunity. There must be something that is happening; people are grossly dissatisfied, they are quitting, you're having a problem attracting candidates, there is a shortage of qualified people to fill jobs from within, et cetera.

Before undertaking a project, you must have a tangible and explainable action/result relationship between the program or activity which is being contemplated and the need or opportunity which has been identified. This action/result criterion is by far the most important of the three. We know that something different isn't necessarily something better; just as change isn't necessarily progress.

The action/result relationship is sometimes difficult to determine with a certainty, but here are two things to consider. First, don't proceed unless you're reasonably certain that the action you are contemplating will have a predictable result which will deal effectively with the problem or opportunity. Second, starting now, build into each project or activity you undertake criteria by which it can later be evaluated. In this way, you will be developing better skills and techniques for determining action/result relationships in the future. Determining better action/result relationships is a major job for personnel in the future.

We should, of course, always determine the cost of a project or activity which is being contemplated. Equally important, however, is to make some estimate of the value of the activity to the firm. Determining values is more difficult than determining cost, but it is the value of activities which is typically the more important of the two variables. Because of the difficulties and the imprecision of both cost and value estimates, I would suggest, as a general rule of thumb, that you never proceed with a project or activity unless the value you estimate is at least four times the anticipated cost.

Consider reorganization of the personnel department. Personnel departments are frequently too compartmentalized. For example, a company might have three people in compensation, four in employment and three in training. Forty percent of personnel work each week or each day is not employment work. Also, if you have four people in the department, the work will expand to fill the time available.

Work to improve the way your time is used. Personnel people must be accessible. On the other hand, the "open telephone" policy can result in great inefficiencies in the use of time. Organize your time, and allocate some of that time when personnel people are not available by phone or for people who happen to drop in while walking down the hall.

Analyze your time. Each personnel professional has an enormous variety of things he does. We know that some are more important than others; some have higher priorities than others. Time actually spent on activities, however, does not necessarily correlate with either the urgency or the importance of items. Keep track of your time, and compare the result with your own sense of importance and urgency of the various items.

Apply the concept of sufficiency. Personnel professionals are sometimes called to "overkill" an item. In staffing, for example, most operating managers would like to see a number of well-qualified people. Why would they need to see more than one well-qualified person? What is the basis for selecting among these well-qualified people?

Use the "low-handicapper" system. If there's a question about the appropriate salary for a job, the salary administrator should answer it. This shouldn't be the subject of meetings and long discussions, including opinions of those who know little about the subject. If the salary administrator is competent, his word should be final.

Zero-base review every personnel program in practice at least once every five years. At least, make a list of all the important and time-consuming activities of the personnel department. Spend half a day each year reviewing part of that list and asking such questions as "Why are we doing this?" and "Is this the most effective way to accomplish our objectives?"

If you haven't started using information systems, this might be an opportunity for increasing the effectiveness of the personnel organization immensely. This is going to be the mode of work within a few years anyway. We may as well start now. By doing so, you will not only be preparing for the future but you will also be increasing the efficiency of your operations today.

The personnel department may do too much for operating units. Many personnel departments today make decisions for operating units that the operating units can make for themselves. This has a double impact upon the effectiveness of work. Personnel people are doing work they needn't do. Also, if the decision of the personnel department is not to the liking of the operating unit, they then spend time defending their decisions.

Take a hard look at the meetings you hold. There probably isn't any unit in a company that spends more of their time in meetings than those in personnel work. We could make a list of companies where the chances are 99 out of 100 that when you try to call someone his secretary will tell you that he's in a meeting. The only way you ever get through to these people is to call them and ask to have your call returned.

There is always the possibility that some work can be eliminated; perhaps because some program or practice is now obsolete. It's really a good idea to put a "sunset date" on every personnel activity. This is a date when the activity would terminate unless there was a review that determined that the practice still serves the interests of the firm.

Make sure that you are constantly realigning personnel support time in each activity in line with current needs. Personnel department time is very high during program development and early implementation stages. The need for personnel department time falls off sharply after the program has been implemented, but it can still be substantial. Within a couple of years, however, the time required by members of the personnel department for ongoing support, explanation, and answering with respect to that activity should diminish sharply. There is, however, a tendency to continue the administrative support even when the needs for support diminish. Make sure that's not happening.

We may also be gearing up in some areas for more help than is needed by our managers. Not many years ago, operating managers knew little about personnel work. Even during the 1960s, it was quite typical to have to explain basic things about personnel work. Today, however, managers have been exposed to personnel activities in their own company, some have taken personnel courses in college, and all have been exposed to a lot of personnel information in the magazines they read. The more they know, the less they need what you know.

LEADERSHIP COMPANIES

The work of the personnel department is better in some firms than in others. All firms can learn from each other, and those who are leadership companies with respect to personnel department work can be particularly instructive.

With this in mind, subscribers to *The Sibson Report* participated in a study to determine just which firms were "leadership companies" in the field of personnel management. The work covered more than a year and results were presented in a number of reports, as well as some Briefs and Special Reports.

One thing we learned was that leadership companies like to maintain a low profile. They don't want to spend time telling other firms what they do, preferring instead to use that time to do it even better. They have no desire to help other firms improve their personnel management; particularly competitor firms. Therefore, to get the information desired it was necessary for us to promise that we would not identify these leadership firms; and we never did. What they did permit, however, was the publication of characteristics or criteria which best reflected personnel work in their firms. There were ten such criteria for leadership work in personnel.

1. Employee productivity is high when compared with comparable firms, and the rate of productivity improvement is better

than in most firms. Personnel work has to do with the effectiveness of people in their work. If a firm does personnel work well, then productivity will be high and/or it will be increasing.

2. Leadership firms are largely nonunion; and/or the percentage of unionized employees as a portion of total employment is declining. Of course, the number of union personnel will vary a great deal with industries, and we know also that the percentage of union members in business overall is declining. But the point is that excellence in personnel management contributes to a nonunion status, that sooner or later it will facilitate decertification of unions that oppose practices that support effective work, and that union organization of new facilities is less likely in leadership companies.

3. A number of managers are recruited from leadership firms to substantially higher-level positions, and they are usually successful in their new jobs. Companies with sound personnel activities produce good managers. Therefore, they will tend to be on the "hit list" of recruiters. It's not likely that managers in leadership firms will leave their jobs unless they are offered a new job that is substantially better. They will get such offers, and those who accept them will likely be successful. Also, leadership firms pay attention to the development of managers and to management succession. Therefore, they will have, at any point in time, an inventory of well-qualified managers; an inventory that would exceed the immediate opportunities available. So, the leadership company is also likely to be vulnerable to having top operations managers recruited to substantially higher-level positions in other firms.

4. When search firms receive assignments to get top-level personnel people, the client company frequently specifies that it would prefer someone from this firm, but is rarely successful in getting him. A leadership firm is good at personnel management, and that firm's personnel professionals are good. Good recruiters will know this. Therefore, personnel

people in a leadership firm will also be on search firms' "hit lists." Unlike operating managers, however, personnel people will not likely leave a leadership company, even for substantially higher-level positions. In leadership firms, personnel people tend to know that they are doing better personnel work; that they are winners. They would be disinclined to move to another firm with a lesser commitment to excellence of the management of personnel. It would take an unusual offer to get them to move.

5. Leadership firms have highly competent personnel people *at all levels*, but these people aren't necessarily well-known in the field. Recognize that there isn't always a correlation between competence at work and fame in a field of work.

6. A leadership company in personnel work is always highly successful. No doubt, at any given point in time there are successful companies that are less than great in personnel management. But high levels of business success without excellence of personnel management are short-lived; over a period of time, only firms with good personnel management will continue to be highly successful.

7. These firms almost never go outside to recruit general management executives or key people in personnel or finance. Part of the excellence of the management of people is to provide a pool of qualified people to fill the needs of the business.

8. These firms are well-regarded in their communities and always have a large backlog of unsolicited "gate applications." These leadership firms are highly regarded as a place to work by their own employees. The company's employees communicate this in many ways to others in the community, who then also seek to work for the company.

9. All managers of people are reasonably conversant with the essentials of personnel management. There is not only excellence of management by operating managers in all areas of

the firm but they all know well the basics of personnel administration.

10. A leadership firm has an inclination for practical innovation in personnel and is willing to allocate resources for the development of new and better methods of managing people. Leadership firms gained excellence in personnel in part by seeking better ways to manage people.

DO BETTER

Learn from the experiences of other personnel departments, but never copy what they do. Be sure you know what they really do, why they did it, and how it worked. Don't get preoccupied with being a leadership company: the goal is business success and not recognition.

Of course, the personnel department wants to do its best; the trouble is we rarely know what our best is. I tend to evaluate the effectiveness of personnel departments in client companies by two criteria: are they doing better now than they did before, and are they doing their personnel work better than their competitors?

If they are doing better than they did before, for a long enough period of time, they will be doing very well. You can measure progress; you can evaluate whether the work is better or not.

So far as doing better than the competition is concerned, I am reminded of a story. Two lions hunters expended their last shot, but it only wounded their prey. The lion glared at them, clearly intent on a charge. The first hunter dropped his rifle and started putting on his track shoes. The second hunter said, "You can't outrun that lion." The first hunter responded, "I don't have to outrun that lion; I only have to outrun you."

Chapter 6

BACK TO THE BASICS

While the size, role, and talent of the personnel organization have increased greatly, a review of the personnel function over the past 35 years suggests to me that some of the basics of personnel have been neglected. Because personnel organizations necessarily focused so much time and attention on new programs, new techniques, and new activities over the past 35 years, some basic personnel activities may have been allowed to deteriorate. Therefore, many companies now need to go back to the basics. The four basic personnel activities which I suggest should be reviewed are: employment, personnel information, labor relations, and the management of compensation costs. The need to go back to the basics is covered here, and more specific comments about each of these areas are in the five succeeding chapters.

LABOR RELATIONS

The need to return to the basics is most apparent with respect to labor relations. In the 1950s through the 1970s, excellence in labor relations eroded badly. For example, pay rates of many unionized workers were increased to a point where they were far in excess of the market; far more than necessary to attract, motivate, and retain the number and quality of people required to do the work. Companies agreed to these high rates because all their competitors negotiated the same high rates, and the thought was that the customers would have to cover the costs. Then in the automobile industry, as one example, came the imports, and people bought new cars less frequently because of "sticker shock."

Highly restrictive work practices became part of labor contracts. There were many of them, and they caused a great decline in productivity. Finally, a strong and destructive adversarial atmosphere in collective bargaining emerged and became ingrained.

Some people think that productivity bargaining and give-back contracts will correct errors committed in prior years in labor relations. Give-back bargaining is more likely a temporary event, brought about by economic circumstances. There is still an adversarial relationship; in the case of give-back bargaining in 1982 and 1983, the company was the winner. In some of these cases, unfortunately in the very period when the company won concessions, it also designed more lucrative bonus arrangements for management and granted key people golden parachute contracts.

Under these circumstances, the period of give-back negotiations will likely be followed by get-back bargaining and then get-even confrontations. In the meantime, profit-sharing plans granted as part of the give-back bargaining will start paying large sums; making some industries still less competitive in world markets. Then we may see many years of recurring give-back/get-back battles. The victims will be workers who lose their jobs and the American public, who will pay a bitter economic price.

There has been and will continue to be compelling reasons to return to the basics in labor relations. Some industries have become uncompetitive in world markets. Companies are going bankrupt. Workers are losing their jobs. The real income of Americans is declining. We can't afford desired social programs. There are a few who benefit from this scenario. Those on Wall Street who arrange mergers of troubled companies get rich; but they are mating dinosaurs.

In a unionized location, collective bargaining is essentially the management of personnel. Often in unionized situations we have the management of personnel at its very worst. We need to bring wages more in line with the market. Hopefully, this can be done over time by "containing" future increases rather than cutting back on pay levels. More importantly, we must continue to remove ineffective work practices and work rules; we must get on with the positive job of productivity bargaining. And perhaps most important of all, if there is to be a permanent improvement in labor relations, a partnership rather than an adversarial relationship must evolve.

EMPLOYMENT

Employment is also a very basic personnel activity. It has to do with the acquisition of assets. It involves the acquisition of our most important assets; the human talent in the company. The erosion in the excellence of the employment activity in firms is less visible than it is in labor relations, but the erosion of excellence has been very great in employment, and only a small part of this is due to governmental regulations.

For example, many companies have virtually delegated the recruiting of executives to recruiting firms. These are outside people who may be very good at finding some kinds of people. But they don't necessarily seek out the best candidates; frequently just those with the best surface credentials. Furthermore, most outside recruiters are not well-qualified to do screening.

One of the most important people in the personnel organization in the 1940s and early 1950s was the college recruiter. Are they as good today? These college recruiters have fallen from number two or three in importance in the personnel organization to number 20 or number 30 in importance. This is symbolic of the erosion of excellence in employment.

Companies often have very low-level people doing recruiting. Some take false comfort in the notion that, even though the recruiters might be junior, those who make the final selections are managers. But the managers select from among those presented to them by these low-level recruiters, and therefore their choices may not be adequate. Employment practices in companies today are not very different than they were 35 years ago. With all the focus on program development, there isn't much that is new or better in recruiting and selecting people brought into the firm. This is one of the few areas where there may be a need for some practical program development work. The increase in technology and government regulations requires the development of more cost-effective recruiting practices and better screening methods.

Perhaps in the past, businesses have been lulled into complacency in employment because they had always paid more than most other types of employers in the marketplace and, therefore, had that competitive advantage. In most jobs, and particularly in technology jobs where the need for more people is the greatest, private firms no longer pay more than employers in other sectors of the economy.

There is intense competition in many job categories; and a need for greater excellence in employment. For example, when unemployment was close to 10 percent in 1982, the "Unfilled Jobs Index" was 5 percent: during a period of recession and high unemployment, one of every 20 jobs in business was not filled.

At the very least, we have "stood still" with respect to the excellence of recruiting and employment. Jobs have become more complex; competition for talent has become more intense. There is a need for a resurgence in the excellence of employment. There is a need to probe new opportunities, such as early identification of talent and career hiring.

INFORMATION

Based upon a number of experiences, I have recently come to believe that there has also been an erosion in the excellence of personnel information. For example, in a number of conferences that I held in Florida participants were asked to bring copies of their regular personnel reports. Some firms did not have such reports and the data in others was sparse, reflecting mostly what the accounting department required. Also, when *The Sibson Report* distributed its general personnel data questionnaire in 1983, many subscribers reported that they were unable to provide requested information without considerable effort and work. This questionnaire requested some of the most basic personnel data, including census count, turnover, and job changes.

Recording and reporting personnel information is a very basic personnel activity. It's basic because we need information as at least one objective input to analyzing personnel situations, for early identification of personnel problems, and as a tool in personnel decision making. Also, personnel information itself can be a factor in improving personnel administration. When managers throughout the organization know that such information is being reported, they will tend to do a better job because they are being monitored.

We need not just return to the basics with respect to personnel information for good personnel management reasons, but also because of the information revolution. Very soon, all companies will be on full-line electronic data processing. This means that everything formerly typed will then go into the electronic information system and be instantly retrievable, on a plain English language basis. The opportunities for the constructive use of information under these circumstances, in a problem-solving and decision-making manner, is enormous. But the users—those in personnel—must identify what is needed and specify the kind of information that should be put into the system.

MANAGING COMPENSATION COSTS

A fourth basic activity of personnel, which has been traditional and managed excellently in the past, is the management of compensation. It was always the goal of companies to ensure that they paid "fairly"; which usually meant that pay for *jobs* should be competitive.

In my opinion, companies should pay salaries which are generally average, compared to the relevant labor markets, unless there is a compelling business reason to do otherwise. We have seen, however, that many companies have pursued a different course. Some have been seduced into setting salaries at the "75th percentile." The reason some follow that course is that they were sold on the idea that if you pay more you get better people; but there is no evidence, either in logic or in experience, to substantiate this view. Surveys have shown, in fact, that three of four firms aim to set salaries for jobs at the 75th percentile. Mathematically, this leads to leveraging up. The result in many cases has been inflated pay; far more than required to attract and retain the number and caliber of people needed to conduct the business.

We have seen even more dramatically how pay has gotten out of line with the needs of the market in recent cases of "deregulation." In the stock brokerage business, airlines, steel, and automobiles, pay in many job categories was set at a rate *far* above competitive levels. The same thing has happened, for different reasons, in many professional, management, and executive jobs.

Some would ask, "What's wrong with paying more than required by the labor markets?" "More is better," is their argument; and for lower-paid people, you can argue correctly that their families need more income. What's wrong, however, is that somebody pays; and mostly it is the lower- and middle-income workers who pay. Furthermore, inflated pay is unfair to those who want the job, need the job, could do the job, and would be very happy to be paid at competitive job rates. Finally, there is the risk of loss of jobs; particularly to foreign competitors. We have seen a lot of that in the past 35 years.

We need to get back to this basic issue also. We need to manage compensation costs. The data for doing so exists; there is far better compensation survey data today than there was 35 years ago. It's simply a job that must be done. We must return to the basics in managing compensation costs.

ONE-DAY-AT-A-TIME MANAGEMENT

We also need to return to the basics in the way we administer personnel activities. So many of our centrally administered programmatic personnel activities are a yearly event, or some other periodic action. Many programs requiring periodic action are necessary or helpful, but they can never take the place of effective management of personnel each day. We must focus more on one-day-at-a-time management of personnel.

In management, we focus too much on one year as a business period; but the time it takes the earth to get around the sun has little relevance to operations in most businesses today. Five-year planning is worse: that has relevance to almost no one. But each day is a relevant business period.

George Burns says that he gets up each morning and feels his pulse first. If it's beating, he has breakfast and gets on with his day. You do somewhat the same; you go to work and get at it each morning. You shut it off when you go home that day. That's a relevant business period.

Even our plans for a *day* don't always work out. Make a list each morning of what you plan to do and see how it works out. You'll see in a few days that unplanned events take more time than planned events. It's good to plan, but recognize that this identifies what you think you'll do; plans represent what you would have done if you hadn't been surprised.

It's what we plan to do each day and get done which represents progress: one step at a time. Much of what is in yearly plans or programs (which are perpetual plans) provides mostly guidance as to which direction to take.

Elsewhere in this book we discuss employee communications and performance appraisal. Appropriately, we cover the big issues; matters of basic approach and policy. At the same time, for example, I think everyone agrees that performance appraisal should be done (and, in fact, for better for worse is done) day by day. It's the reactions to what you do each day by your supervisor or by your peers or by managers other than your supervisor which represent the essence of true performance appraisal.

Advocates of traditional performance appraisal say that it is of value to summarize all these reactions and experiences into a once-each-year formal appraisal. Even if such summarizations were accurate and useful, however, no one I know would disagree that it is the day-by-day experiences that represent real performance appraisal.

All the material generated by company-initiated communications represents only a fraction of the real communications which take place at work. Real communications are what an employee is told on the job and what he observes on the job. In fact, if your company media communications differ from what people are told and experience each day, then the company-initiated communications are not believable and there will be a credibility gap.

Companies continue to be inclined to use company-initiated training programs. Some of them are useful and necessary. But we also know that the overwhelming amount of training and development that really occurs in any firm happens day by day in the work place. We are told how to do something; we are shown a better way. We are given instructions. We learn something from observing what others do.

At least in the field of the management of personnel, one-day-at-a-time management is the essence of management. All of our company programs and practices really need to be designed to support that day-by-day management. One-day-at-a-time management of personnel is basic to effective work and needs more attention. Part of the virtue of a delegative approach to the management of personnel is that it focuses more attention, effort, and talent on one-day-at-a-time management.

RESPONSIBILITY FOR THE BASICS

It is extremely important to note that management has, in differing degrees, delegated responsibility and authority for these fundamental personnel activities to outsiders. For example, many companies have delegated their labor relations work to lawyers. Many have delegated at least the recruiting of higher-level people to those in outside search firms. Less directly but sometimes just as meaningfully, companies have delegated the job of managing compensation costs to consultants who focus on surveying. Companies take what the surveyors report as the truth and gear their own pay levels to those reported by the consultants. In the area of information, companies have largely delegated the job of personnel information to accountants and MIS experts.

Basic personnel activities should be the responsibility of those in the personnel department. Companies should pay lawyers for legal advice, not substantive work in labor relations. Companies can do most of their own recruiting, even at the highest levels. If they do use recruiters, the management of the recruiter and the screening of the candidate must be the responsibility of qualified personnel persons. It is cost efficient to have third parties conduct surveys for all; but the users should control the work. With respect to personnel information, personnel persons should determine what information should be kept for purposes of the management of personnel, and they should have complete and instant access to such information.

Chapter 7

LABOR RELATIONS

I am not a labor relations technician. I never negotiated a union contract during my consulting career; primarily because I think only company people should sit at the bargaining table. Therefore, my role with clients involved policy mattters, strategy, and advice; so that's all I can contribute here.

Rarely did I do union avoidance work. My focus was on effective personnel management and the effective management of personnel. If those things are done well, then let the workers make the choice. There are also some of us who believe strongly that unions are a vital part of American business, so I generally did not want to be involved in union avoidance. Someone has to represent the collective views of workers. I don't think top management can, and I want the government to stay out. Unions are the only other choice. As a result, the only union avoidance work I did was in enterprises like hospitals; where the right to strike might mean the right to kill.*

Labor relations is a basic part of personnel. In unionized

---

*There is a great need for effective legislation governing public emergency strikes. It isn't a question of strikes against government agencies, but any strike that causes great harm to the general public instead of the parties. In a civilized society, one simply cannot tolerate strikes that may kill, cause civil disorders, deprive any family of the necessities of life, or impair national security. When you take away the right to strike, you must have an alternate method of assuring equity in terms of wages, benefits, and conditions of work for employees. I suggest methods for doing this in *Common Sense Answers* (scheduled for publication in 1986), but I would welcome your answers to this critically important issue.

companies it is largely the management of personnel. It has to do with the excellence of work and the effectiveness of work. Therefore, labor relations must be done well. I have some standard advice for executives in unionized operations on this matter and will summarize it here.

I recommend that top executives should hold a summit meeting on labor relations. It can last for only a day. Have your chief executive officer, perhaps some members of your board of directors, senior executives of the operations, and your personnel vice president attend this meeting. Invite the president of each union that represents any employee of the company.

Start by telling these union presidents the truth about how you feel about unions. Let them know that if you had your way there wouldn't be any unions in your company at all. Tell them you don't like unions, and tell them why. Most companies don't like unions because they don't want the risk of strikes and they don't want interference with managers' right to manage. Tell them you recognize that unions are a part of the business scene. They are a reality. Tell them you have been advised (by Bob Sibson, if you like) that someone will represent the collective interests of employees. If it's not unions, it is likely to be the government. If that's your choice, tell them that you welcome these union presidents with open arms as your brothers and sisters.

In this spirit of brotherhood, let them know that you called this meeting to set a new tone for collective bargaining and labor relations. Tell them what you want in the labor relations relationship. Tell them that you would also like to hear what they want. Let's put it all out front.

I recommend that you tell them you want three things—and that you really must have them. These three are essential: they are things you must have. If you do not get them, then, regrettably, there must be a war.

Tell these union presidents that you will do anything legal and proper to achieve these objectives; but, of course, only say that if you mean it. Tell them that if it takes a strike to achieve these three essential objectives there will be strikes, and they can last forever. If there has to be work toward decertification, then that will happen. If you have to go through bankruptcy to achieve these objectives, you will do it. You will do anything legal to get

94

these three essential issues; because you think the business has to have them. You have to have them now or later; and you are out to get them now, while you still have the resources to fight a war, if that's what it takes.

All that should get their attention. Now tell them about the three essential things you think the company must have in its relations with unions. Here are the three I would suggest.

First of all, tell them that you must have a productive work force. This is essential. There can't be any unproductive work practices at all—none!

In fact, tell them you think that every employee, union or nonunion, should be expected to do his job as best he can. Each person who works in the company, including its executives, should give 100 percent every day. Furthermore, tell these union presidents that you think it is the job of every person and every group of people who work in the firm to seek out and determine more efficient ways to work.

Tell them that you will do anything necessary to get a productive work force because you think it is essential for survival, let alone success. Tell them that you are a businessman who will do whatever is necessary to achieve essential business objectives—that's your job. For example, tell them you would take a $20 a share charge to earnings to shut down a losing business; and you would do the same thing to stop unproductive business practices which ultimately will shut down all the businesses. Tell them that you expect this attitude of a 100 percent effort and a constant searching for better ways to work to become a part of the culture of the business.

Second, I would urge you to tell these union presidents that you want to pay competitively; no less and no more. Perhaps the union or your personnel department may be able to badger you into 10 percent more than the market, because you know that the statistics on what is competitive aren't that great anyway. But never will you agree to 20 percent above market averages.

By paying competitively, tell them that you mean an amount equal to the statistical average of other jobs in the labor markets. That's sufficient to attract and retain the number of fully qualified people necessary to run the business. Tell them that it is your view that paying competitively is paying fairly.

Point out that your company simply cannot be uncompetitive in a market sense. No longer can companies delude themselves, for example, into thinking that as long as every firm in an industry is uncompetitive in the market the customer will simply have to pay the price. The customers have shown that they will find another way; either a different way to spend their money or someplace else to spend it, like Japan. Tell them that as an American you are tired of jobs being exported. As a businessman, you won't run the risk or the vulnerability of loss of business and loss of jobs which are inherent in being uncompetitive in the labor market.

Of course, let them know that when the company has an especially good year it should share the results of that success with all employees (not just executives). There are many ways to do this, and perhaps your company has some now. If not, you should consider them. But what you won't consider, under any circumstances, is to build into the fixed costs of your company wages that are higher than competitive in the market. It is right to pay competitively from the business point of view; it is also morally the right thing to do.

Third, I would suggest that you tell these union presidents that you will no longer have an adversarial relationship with unions. Perhaps at this point, you should symbolically put your hand out to tell them, with a gesture, that you no longer consider them your enemies. But tell them also that you will not work with any who think of you as their enemy. Tell them that you repent for any of your past sins and that now you want to work in a partnership manner with all employees and with the unions that represent employees.

Having pointed out the three essential things that you must have, you would subsequently tell them that there is, of course, plenty of room for discussion of the conditions under which these are achieved. There is no intention to be inflexible or dictatorial about how these vital company goals are to be achieved. Simply tell them that you want to be up-front and honest, and let them know that you must have these three essential items and why they are critical.

You might not want to get into it at the meeting but, for example, you want greater productivity. On the other hand, if I

96

were you, I'd be inclined to accept the condition that no employee will ever lose his or her job because of productivity improvement actions. You want to be competitive, but if I were you, I would be inclined to accept "wage containment" to get there rather than wage cuts.

Now you wait for a reaction. How do you think unions would react to these statements on the part of company executives—assuming, of course, that they really believe you meant what you said?

Rarely have union leaders in this country sought unproductive practices or inefficient work. They do want more; more than competitive pay, including wonderful benefits and improved working conditions, which sometimes means easier work. But I'm not sure that they want these things to the point that they would have an all-out war. Don't we all want more? But hopefully, we all have also learned some practical economics from the experiences of the past 35 years. We know that competitively we can't eat that cake and have our jobs too.

Hopefully, your union presidents, as well as yourselves, will recognize that "labor" and "management" are not the main protagonists anymore, if ever they were. All workers in a firm have a common cause—their collective success. The enemies are the foreign firms; and I fear increasingly that the major protagonists are workers versus nonworkers.

Having told them what you want, now ask them what they want. Ask them what issues are essential from a union point of view— to the point that they would go to war.

They may come up with something that you haven't thought of, but I suspect that if you get what you want it would be difficult to imagine anything that unions want seriously that you would not find acceptable. So ask them not to be bashful. You weren't bashful about telling the unions what you wanted, in the sense that you had to have them. Tell them now that you want to hear what they want, in the sense that they feel they have to have them.

You might be surprised at the things they say they want. And you might be even more surprised at what they don't say they want.

I have heard what unions want and the things they think are essential. But I have experienced too few cases to report them with comfort. Rather, I would like to urge any reader whose company follows this course to let me know what unions say they must have. And, of course, if there are any union readers, I would certainly welcome their comments as to the things that unions want, in the sense that they feel they must have them. If I get a sufficient amount of such material to draw relevant conclusions, the material will be the subject of a future section in *The Sibson Report*.

When you hear these essential union expectations or demands, you should naturally expect that they too will be willing to discuss the conditions. How you reach these critical items is something that will then be a matter for serious, but constructive, collective bargaining.

You could accomplish this whole discussion in one day. If you reach an agreement and an open understanding with your union presidents on what is critical to the company and what is critical to them, then you have accomplished a great deal. It would be the basis for the effective management of personnel among unionized workers for many years into the future. It would be the basis for continuing improvement in the effectiveness of work. It would do much to stop the loss of jobs; we may even import some jobs from Taiwan. And it would do wonders for the climate of work.

I also recommend a one-day management meeting. There are some essential management practices which must be determined and implemented if we are to have more effective labor relations. Each firm needs to determine its own agenda items. However, there are four management decisions which I think should be on every firm's list.

You have already told the union presidents that the end of the adversarial relationship is essential. But it takes two sides to make peace. The CEO should make it plain to all managers that, for its part, the company is going to give the new spirit of collective bargaining its best shot. It was the company's suggestion to end the adversarial relationship; the company should take the initiative to make it happen. Be affirmative in these actions. Assume there is a constructive and cooperative relationship now. Don't ever think negatively. And no more references to those "bleeping" union leaders.

My second recommendation for management action in labor relations is to do a little reorganizing. One of the worst errors ever made in the field of personnel was to separate labor relations from personnel management; a company's version of the Marine Corps and the Peace Corps. The job is the effective management of personnel; some do personnel work with union workers, others with nonunion workers, and some with both. Combine labor relations and personnel. Call it what you like. But the organization that does personnel work can reasonably be called the personnel department.

Some with labor relations training and experience will have to be retrained, and not all will make the transition successfully. Many personnel generalists will similarly need to learn about labor relations. If, in the process, they come to understand American working men and women better, the excellence of personnel would be improved greatly.

Next, I urge the CEO to set a very important objective: limit every union contract to six pages. Make it six pages, double spaced, and insist that it be written in the English language so everyone will be able to read it.

A six-page document will describe what the union and the company agree to. Long, detailed agreements identify a lot of things the parties can disagree about. Keep it short, and make it simple.

Lawyers will tell you that such a document would not be a legally enforceable contract. That's but one of the many advantages of a six-page contract. Such a document is not likely to be the basis of arbitration either; and that's another advantage. In this way, the union and company must work out everything themselves. In my opinion, a major management policy would be never go to court and never go to arbitration. Arbitrators and judges don't know anything about the management of personnel; and you get the impression that they never heard of the word productivity. Lawyers don't know much about these matters either.

The fourth management action which I think should always be listed is to keep out the lawyers. Keep them out of labor relations altogether. Never have a lawyer sit at the collective bargaining table. Never involve a lawyer in a grievance procedure.

Never have lawyers write the contract—they can't write in the English language anyway. With respect to the management of personnel, at least, lawyers really should confine themselves to providing legal advice.

Chapter 8

STAFFING

Of all the personnel management practices which determine the excellence of the management of personnel, none is as important as staffing. When we recruit people into the firm, we are acquiring the human assets of the firm; the firm's most important assets. Internal recruiting is no less important: it has to do with asset utilization and the development of those critical human assets. For those who work in the firm, internal recruitment has to do with career progress and the pay progress which goes with it, which are first in importance among employee objectives.

PUT YOUR PERSONNEL DOLLARS UP-FRONT

Those introductory statements seem so obvious that they may appear to waste space and your reading time. But review your staffing procedures anyway. Do those procedures square with the importance of staffing? In most firms I know, the answer would clearly be no.

One of the most fundamental truths of personnel management is to "put your personnel dollars up-front." This means that we should spend the effort and the money in the proper recruiting of people into the firm in the first place. If we hire people who are suitable for the work and who are inclined to do their best, then we will have productive levels of work. Improved effectiveness in recruiting is, in fact, the most productive productivity improvement program. If we hire those who are self-motivated, good learners, and inclined toward self-development, then the

CARL A. RUDISILL LIBRARY
LENOIR-RHYNE COLLEGE

need for training and development is substantially less. If we hire the correct proportion of high-potential people, succession is not a problem. And so it goes with all facets of personnel management. An effective job of hiring the proper human resources in the first instance makes much of what we do in personnel far easier and much more effective. An inadequate job of recruiting makes effective personnel work impossible.

STAFFING TOOLS

You could write a book about all the tools, techniques, and practices which are available for recruiting people into the firm and selecting them for promotion within the firm, and many people have. We also have as much experience and good precedents in staffing as in any other facet of personnel. Recruiting was one of the first activities in personnel.

We have developed many useful and usable techniques in outside recruiting and in selection for promotion. We have tests that are highly useful and usable, interviewing techniques which can be very effective, reference checks, and other methods. We don't lack methodology, know-how, or practices. But if there were ever a place in personnel where the old adage about not farming half as well as we know how to applies, it is with respect to staffing.

I would particularly urge companies to pay attention to the recruiters. If you do excellent selection from among candidates who aren't terribly well-qualified to begin with, then excellent selection methods will still result in bad staffing. All company recruiters don't have to be "high-level"; their level should be somewhat the same as those being recruited. They must know something about the jobs to be filled. They must have certain personal qualities; including great energy and salesmanship.

Companies also need to analyze their recruiting experiences to make sure they know the recruiting source that is most effective for each type of job. In addition to the overall human resources information system, a firm must develop certain special personnel data. One such special information system, which will pay for itself many times over, is an ongoing data system for monitoring the cost-effectiveness of different sources for jobs where there is substantial recruiting. That data should include measures of the subsequent job success of those recruited.

I also think that many companies rely too much on outside recruiters. I think they use them more often than they need to; and when they use them, they rely on them too much. Getting the right supply of candidates before those who make the selection is critical and cannot be abdicated to an outsider. Large firms should even consider establishing their own in-house recruiting organization for management and professional persons. Any firm that averages more than ten searches a year would save money by following this course. You don't need a separate unit. It's better to have a project organization and deploy the man hours when you have openings to fill. You might also have an inventory of outside candidates for key jobs. Get their names from your own employees.

Then organize for effective screening and selection. The manager of personnel must have the basic responsibility for hiring, and if the job is structured as I have recommended, he will have the time and know-how to do this critical job well. The recruiter is part of the project team. There also should be a person from the personnel organization involved in the process. I like to see a third screener-selector in the selection project organization. The best project group should be determined for each job to be filled.

With respect to every job to be filled, conduct an in-house search *first*; before you start outside recruiting. Do internal recruiting by having the personnel department make an in-house search *and* by "posting" the job opening in some appropriate manner. Screen and assess every candidate. Even if you don't find a qualified person inside your firm, you have accomplished two goals. First, you looked, and employees will know you looked inside before looking outside. Second, your best-qualified internal candidates provide a standard against which you evaluate candidates from the outside; and people brought in from the outside must be clearly better than your best internal candidates.

Each member of the project group has a special responsibility. The recruiter gets good candidates; quickly and at the lowest cost. Personnel persons focus their interview on general qualities that are important to the job and the company, such as intelligence, personal goals, and personal qualities. The personnel generalist also sees to other vital aspects of the selection process; e.g., required testing, checking on the person's prior record, and conformance to EEO requirements. The manager of personnel focuses his interview on job know-how; and he might have a working associate interview for this purpose also. Their focus is on "work sample interviewing." The "other" member of the project group should conduct a very open interview. When the final selection decision is made, the "other" member should play the role of a "devil's advocate," an extra check on the appropriateness of the final selection decision.

What has been outlined here is a "basic" selection process. Don't add to that process unless there will be a provable value from any other selection activity. Remember, you must do a quality job; but it must also be done quickly. Don't do more than is sufficient. It increases costs, spreads the elapsed time of hire, and may add nothing to the excellence of recruiting.

Our recruiting is not always as good as it should be; our selection procedures are sometimes worse. A few years ago, for example, I embarrassed a client company; although my purpose was to have them do some constructive work in interviewer training. What I had them do was to identify the six managers at a large location who were the most skilled and experienced employment interviewers. With the agreement of these people and those being interviewed, we taped three interviews by each manager, thinking we would take the best three of all the interviews and use them as a model. Other supervisors could listen to these taped cases and learn to become better interviewers. What we found was that the best interviewers were terrible.

For example, they spent more than half their time talking rather than listening. They spent more than half of the remaining time asking information that was already available from some other source, such as the employment application form. There was great redundancy; asking questions that had already been answered or covering information that had been covered in other interviews. On the average, only three minutes in every hour of interviewing time was used in getting information that was useful in evaluating the applicant's suitability for the job. And these were the best interviewers.

Of course, we know how to interview better than that; and those managers could do it better. But they didn't. Generally speaking, they hadn't prepared for the interview; they hadn't given thought to what relevant questions to ask; and in every case, in fact, they had done so little interviewing in the prior year that it was not surprising that their skills had been dulled.

Companies that appoint managers of personnel should at least deal with the issue of sufficient time and sufficient practice in interviewing so the job can be done well. But companies also need to pay attention to such basics as organizing a screening process so different interviewers can focus on different subjects.

I would hope that this simple illustration makes the point that the first thing to do is to make better use of the basic tools that are available in recruiting, staffing, and selection, either with respect to external recruiting or promotion from within. Of course, selection will never be a perfect process, but in many firms there is a great opportunity to improve the excellence of staffing enormously and at almost no cost.

VERTICAL STAFFING

Another critically important point in effective staffing involves the issue of vertical versus horizontal recruiting. In horizontal recruiting, we are selecting a person for a job who has already done the job or a job very similar to the job being filled. In vertical recruiting, we are considering people who have not done the current job but who have been successful in lower-level jobs and are qualified for the position that is open. Vertical recruiting is what always happens with respect to promotion from within. I think vertical recruiting should also be done in external placement.

I think that vertical recruiting is so important that it should be a policy management item. Exceptions to vertical recruiting from outside should be a rarity. It is such an important matter that exceptions should be approved by the highest levels of management.

Too often, when a job is filled from outside, the manager who is accountable for the job wants a person who has already done that work. In this way, the manager feels that the candidate has "proven capability" because he has done it. That's logical thinking but it's usually an error. For one thing, you should ask, "Why would a person who has already successfully done a job want to do it again?" "How much of a compensation premium will you have to pay to get such a person?" "Are you sure that the person did the job well or is he, in fact, willing to accept a position in the same level because he has been asked, however subtly, to leave his present job?"

Vertical recruiting is more difficult, both in terms of identifying candidates and selecting them. But the track records of those recruited vertically are so much better and the compensation costs are so much less that it's worth the extra investment in staffing excellence. Keep in mind the rule of thumb that one dollar more in annual compensation costs is equivalent to five dollars more in one-time recruiting.

FUTURE NEEDS

Companies are well-advised to look carefully at the issue of staffing because it is so critical to the effective management of personnel. It is one of the basics that many companies have neglected under the pressure of so many new tasks. It is also important to review staffing because companies need to achieve a higher level of excellence in staffing in the future.

In the near future, companies may find greater difficulty in recruiting and, therefore, greater demands on the staffing activity because of greater competition for available talent. Traditionally, businesses have been advantaged in labor markets, primarily because they offered premium pay in most job categories. Increasingly, nonbusiness enterprises, and especially governmental agencies, provide total pay at least equal to the average paid in business. At the same time, the nonbusiness sector of the economy is growing more rapidly than many long-established sectors of the private economy. There will be more and more demand from labor market competitors for people to fill many jobs, and they will be paying fully competitive amounts. Thus in the future, business faces a situation where there will be more competitors for available talent but business will not have a competitive pay advantage.

Companies will also have to develop new types of recruiting skills. One of these involves what is referred to now as "career selection."

In the past, employees frequently changed jobs and changed employers, but almost all spent their entire working lives in one job career. In the next 35 years, it will become quite common for people to change job careers at least once. Companies that want to move personnel into different career paths within the firm will have to look for "transference capabilities" when they bring people into the company.

People are changing jobs within the firm more frequently. Companies that select an applicant solely on the basis of his ability to do an open job are not considering the fact that employees stay on that job, at most levels, for approximately three years; but they will stay with a company for an average of ten years.

More and more, companies will have to be looking for raw talent rather than simply qualifications to perform a given job. Basic qualities, such as intelligence and adaptability, are obviously more difficult to assess than tangible qualifications, such as drafting ability. Regarding the impact of computers on business oprations, it's been said that we may never have "smart computers" but that we surely need smarter people to use the computers we have.

In some cases, companies will have to pay more attention to "early identification" in their selection of people who come into the company. For example, management will be enhancing its subsequent success in management succession activities if it selects people who can be identified early in their careers, by work they have done and things they have accomplished prior to coming to the company, as having the basic capabilities predictive of success as managers in the future. There is now some evidence that the qualities that are essential for success in executive management work manifest themselves in middle college years.

Finally, of course, there will be increasing government constraints that will have to be considered in the employment process. We should expect the government to become more concerned about the validity of selection processes and whether they serve a positive purpose or are, in fact, discriminatory. The government is also likely to be equally interested and aggressive in ensuring nondiscriminatory practices with respect to promotion from within as they have been with respect to employment of people from outside the firm. And with the continuing desire to improve the social environment, new requirements not yet considered by Congress are always a likelihood.

MANPOWER MANAGEMENT

One future development which is certain, in my opinion, is that staffing as an activity in the personnel department will become an integral part of a "manpower management" function. The traditional functional areas of activities in personnel that would likely be a part of "manpower management" would include:

- Recruiting
- Selection, including testing and interviewing
- Internal staffing and transfers
- Organizational structuring
- Manpower controls
- Communications
- Job structuring and job redesign
- Safety and medical services

With this breadth of activities, manpower management would be one of the major functional areas of personnel. It would stand alongside such other major areas as compensation and benefits (plus HRIS management), manpower development (e.g. training and development plus succession), and corporate relations.

The essential reason for evolving the manpower management function is that the specific areas of activities clustered under this function are very closely interrelated. Of course, all areas of personnel impact each other. Some, however, are so interrelated that they represent different facets of one generic activity.

For example, companies must fill openings. That is the generic job. Increasingly, jobs that become open in management, professional, middle-level, and many technical operations-level positions have, over a period of time, been tailored or customized to the individuals who filled them. It is not true that the "man makes the job," but rather that the experiences and proven capabilities of each individual increasingly influence the assignments he receives and his ability to work in concert with others. In today's work environment, when an existing job becomes open, work assignments should properly be reviewed. Rather than simply cloning jobs, there needs to be a redesigning of jobs and an organizational restructuring when such openings occur.

Furthermore, as people are considered for jobs, the particular background of a desired candidate might also suggest some organizational or job structure change in order to utilize that person's skill and knowledge. Today, companies match jobs to people as well as people to jobs.

No longer are the dynamics of organization such that jobs to be filled and the systems for filling them are the fixed and rigid culture suggested by job descriptions and organization charts. There are a multiplicity of ways in which jobs can be designed and organizations structured; and this must be influenced by the background and capability of candidates available to fill these positions. Thus the management of manpower is a dynamic activity, carried on at the operational level by location managers and supported by location personnel organizations. These organizations, however, must be supported at the division and corporate levels by staff experts with special knowledge, experience, and expertise in all facets of manpower management.

Chapter 9

PERSONNEL INFORMATION

Back in the early 1960s when I initiated what I believe was the first organized effort at developing human resources information systems, one of the findings of the first phase of that project was the identification of over 200 personnel data items kept by at least one of the two dozen firms that were in the project group. No doubt, a count of personnel data items today would be much greater; if for no other reason than the increased requirements for recordkeeping by the government. All of that personnel recordkeeping costs a substantial amount of money. Some of the information can be of high value. Work on personnel information is one of the basics of effective personnel.

THE NEED FOR PERSONNEL INFORMATION

In work on personnel information it is helpful to think about three types of data. The first type of personnel data involves information that the company must keep because it is in business. Second there is data which must be kept for reasons of government compliance. Third, there is information which might be kept for purposes of the improved management of personnel.

A firm must obviously keep some data just because it is in business. It must, for example, know those who work in the firm. The company must know how much it pays each of these people. It must keep information such as date of hire for use in certain benefit plans. The company must know the jobs that people hold and where they work. There is a considerable amount of such information which must be kept because you are in business. Much of this data is used in the accounting department. For this reason I have always referred to information required because a business exists as human resources bookkeeping.

With respect to human resources bookkeeping, a company is well-advised to keep as little data as necessary. It's a good idea to require that the need for human resources bookkeeping data be proven; in the sense that absence of data would impair the conduct of the business. Make sure that such required human resources bookkeeping data is kept on a cost-effective basis. It doesn't matter where such data resides. It could logically be kept in the accounting department, but it must be accessible by personnel people.

In addition to human resources bookkeeping data, there is an increasingly large amount of personnel data which is legally required. A company must maintain and provide a great deal of personnel data to local, state, and federal governments. Companies must also have information to report when questioned or audited.

With respect to this government required human resources bookkeeping data, see your lawyers. Determine from them the minimum amount of legally required data you must keep and don't keep any more than that. Like human resources bookkeeping information, handle government required information in the most cost-effective manner possible.

The third level of personnel information need involves human resources information systems.* This is information for management. Human resources information systems work is not required, but it represents an opportunity. Much of the human resources bookkeeping data and personnel data kept for the gov-

---

*A fourth type of personnel information has been suggested from time to time. This has been referred to as human resources accounting. The objective was to establish a complete set of bookkeeping accounts with respect to personnel in the company. Some universities spent considerable effort trying to develop balance sheets and income statements of employee values. I personally think, however, that such efforts will never be successful; if for no other reason than there will never be a way to account for human assets.

ernment can be kept so that it is usable in human resources information systems work.

HUMAN RESOURCES INFORMATION SYSTEMS

A human resources information system can serve a number of specific objectives of management. For one thing, it can be used as a diagnostic tool; assisting both line management and staff personnel persons to evaluate the health of employee relations in a company.

Second, such a system might identify changes that are occurring which will impact the effective management of human resources and thereby the achievement of business results. In this sense, a human resources information system represents an "early warning system" for management. By identifying emerging problems, solutions that involve a low cost and high effectiveness might then be designed and implemented in a timely manner.

HRIS may also provide basic measures of enterprise performance. These may include productivity measures, manpower ratios, information as to the appropriateness of the organization's structure, and inputs into understanding employee perceptions and attitudes. These are proxy measures of long-term business results. Productivity increases, for example, will usually not impact this year's earnings but will almost inevitably have a profound effect upon the long-term success of the company.

A human resource information system can also provide important data with respect to the degree to which the reasonable aspirations of employees are being fulfilled. Such measures were suggested as a basic need in creating an employee-partner work environment. That data can best be provided by an ongoing human resources information system.

A human resources information system may assist operating managers and personnel people in diagnosing and solving specific personnel problems. The information system itself will never answer questions. It can, however, provide an objective basis for management decisions.

Finally, a human resources information system, as indicated in the description of delegative management, is a critical part of the ongoing process of quality management; which makes delegative management methods practical. The human resources information system provides data which represents an ongoing personnel audit.

There is almost an endless amount of information which might be usable in some way or to some degree in decision making and planning human resources management. But collecting, maintaining, and reporting all of this information involves a cost. Thus this project, like all personnel projects, must not only serve a business need (improved management of personnel) but it must also have a clear action/result effect and be cost effective.

The key to achieving these objectives is in two basic questions. First, what management decisions or management actions would be improved, supported, or likely have more reliability if personnel information which is not now used were available. The development of both operational (yearly) and strategic (more than one year) plans would be an example of management actions which are done better when certain types of personnel information are available.

Much of the information for management purposes will, however, be used by the personnel department. Clearly in this category would be information necessary for the personnel audit. Here also be careful to be highly selective. Be certain that the information itself will be contributive; and that the values will be far greater (at least four times greater) than the cost.

In essence, I am urging that a company take a user's view in developing human resources information systems for management purposes. Too often the focus has been on the technology, the equipment, and the systems. The real issue is what information will contribute to more effective management of people; and this can only be answered by examining the job of management and those in the personnel department.

AN INFORMATION SYSTEM

To develop a human resource information system, a company must set up a uniform chart of accounts for personnel information throughout the company. Every division, every location, and every unit of the company must keep required personnel data in a prescribed manner. This would be one of the requirements in the guidelines component of delegative management.

Personnel information is a bottom-up process. Data is collected and reported at the lowest level of the organization where records are kept. Then it may be combined at each subsequent organizational unit upward until there is a composite corporate information reporting. To do this, however, a uniform chart of accounts is critical. A uniform chart of accounts is important also because companies reorganize and move people around.

There will also be some required personnel practices which are essential to an effective human resources information system. Two examples should illustrate this point. A company must have a single salary structure throughout the organization for information purposes; it must have the same number of grades and the same between-grade progression. Similarly, all performance ratings throughout the firm should be done in the same way.

How human resource information is used is critical to the relevance of the system. Absolute numbers rarely have much significance. Personnel information takes on greater relevance, for example, when viewed comparatively. For example, if a personnel ratio is now 1.0 and was 0.8 not many years ago, the change may be more relevant than either number. The lower ratio which existed before suggests that the personnel department may have become too large. Such comparisons require analysis. For example, you need to determine whether the personnel department is required to do more work today. Also, you must judge whether the personnel department was effective when its ratio was only 0.8.

Trends in personnel information can be even more relevant than prior data. Trends not only indicate prior experience but direction. For example, the corporate office payroll as a percentage of total payroll may be trending up constantly for a number of years. This suggests the possibility that the corporate staff is becoming bloated. Such trends must also be analyzed. The larger corporate staff may, for example, reflect increased governmental requirements.

Personnel data may also be valuable by comparing information about one unit against other units. Personnel results achieved by some units may reflect what can be achieved by others. Here, comparability of the operating units is critical. An ideal case would be a motel chain. Essentially, in many motels every unit is about the same. Then variations in significant personnel data can have relevance; and be the clue toward personnel actions to improve business results in many units. Even in this case, however, further analysis is necessary. While all motels may be the same in terms of size, structure, and operation, their circumstances may still vary. They operate in different geographic regions and are influenced by different economic conditions.

Some companies have also started to build personnel data models. This is a relatively new activity in human resources information systems. The purpose is to determine, through various types of analyses, an ideal that is attainable with respect to certain personnel information. For example, there might be a model of expected distribution of salary increases, which would provide a frame of reference for operating units. There is a danger in such models, however; they may become requirements rather than references.

In some cases it may be necessary to use more than one comparison method to achieve an objective. Also, combination data can be extremely useful. Combination data utilizes two data inputs in your analysis. For example, you might determine the quits among high-performance people.

This outline of comparison methods also indicates a sound process in using personnel data. In human resources information work the personnel professional will observe a trend or comparison that seems important. Then that personnel professional must do some analysis. This may require looking at other data. There may be a need for additional information. After such an analysis, however, the personnel person must always investigate the matter personally before drawing conclusions or taking actions.

When personnel information is handled electronically, this capacity to analyze, to call up more data, to analyze further, and to make various types of comparative studies will increase enormously. Personnel professionals will be able to make analyses in a few minutes that now take days. In the future, this will increase the demand on the ability and the intelligence of personnel professionals in the use of personnel information.

DATA ELEMENTS

A company can have a usable human resources information system with fewer than two dozen items of personnel data input. Experience suggests strongly that companies entering the personnel information area focus on the quality of the information and its usability rather than quantity. You can drown in personnel data. You will have those who will tend to want more and more data: I call them "informaniacs."

Start with the data elements you know you will need and which you keep for business or government requirements. Input this carefully selected data in a way in which you can be assured that it will have maximum usability in subsequent analyses, problem identification, and problem solving. To the extent possible, collect information by using definitions that have already been established; e.g. the government's definition of turnover. In other words, start as simply as possible.

With respect to data items selected, give attention to the possibility that you will subsequently make interbusiness comparisons. Comparisons between businesses in your company are important now. Many believe that personnel data comparisons with other companies will be an important new personnel tool in the immediate future. Avoid, to the extent possible, developing a system that will have to be reworked to make general personnel data comparisons with others in the future.

As you gain experience with the system, there will no doubt be cases where additional data would be clearly helpful in the management of personnel. You should only add such data when the need is clear and the addition of personnel information (the personnel action) will have a clear and predictable contribution to more effective management of personnel (the personnel result). Make certain also that the value of the information will far exceed the cost of inputting it into the information system.

The data inputs are obviously very different and very unique with each company. This is particularly true in the early stages, where you will be well-advised to be highly selective with respect to the data you input into the system and to start by using data you now record. It might, however, be helpful to companies in determining items for collection (input) to see at least one case of how data was subsequently used (the output).

Last year, *The Sibson Report* conducted an interindustry personnel data comparison. Initially, there were 50 companies in this personnel data exchange. The objective was to prove the practicality of such an information exchange of general personnel data and to develop the basic methodologies. Thus this work was designed to be simple; to be a sound first step. There were, nevertheless, a considerable number of data items resulting from this work. Here are those data items.

- Productivity data index; based upon total payroll as percentage of sales.

- The trend of the cost of management; based upon a ratio of management salaries to sales.

- Hire and quit ratios; reported separately for the management group, exempt employees, salaried employees, and hourly employees.

- The number of organizational levels; reported by size of company.

- Supervisory ratios; the average ratio of number of employees per supervisor, reported by size of firm.

- Performance ratings; on a five-gradient basis and reported separately for management, exempt, and salaried persons.

- Potential ratings; again on a five-gradient system, but reported for management only.

- Hiring costs; as a percentage of starting salary.

- Salary increase distribution; reported separately for management, exempt, salaried, and hourly persons.

- Salary level distribution.

- Unfilled job index; the ratio of open requisitions, at a point in time, to total employment, reported separately for management, exempt, salaried, and hourly jobs.

- Personnel ratios; the ratio of personnel to total employment and payroll.

- The number of regulatory cases handled per 1000 employees.

- Consultants' expenses (excluding conferences, legal fees, and actuarial expenses); as a percentage of the total salaried payroll of the personnel department.

- The ratio of promotions to outside hires.

- The total number of job changes as a percentage of employment.

It should be noted that all of this data was reported from information which was obtained from a six-page questionnaire. The questionnaire was designed so that it could be completed in two hours. However, only companies that had a personnel data system could do this. Not one of the 50 companies completed every part of the questionnaire. Most reported that it took much longer than two hours; which indicated that most who participated still had much work to be done in developing their human resources information system. Many firms that did not participate in the work could not do so because of inadequacies of personnel data systems.

INTERBUSINESS COMPARISONS

The general personnel data work conducted by *The Sibson Report* was designed basically to determine whether such work was feasible and whether the results would be useful. That work clearly showed affirmative answers; and indicated that it won't be long before companies will routinely be making interbusiness comparisons of personnel data.

Such work will have a double use. Many companies are, of course, now in multiple business areas. They will want to make such comparisons within their own business. They will also want to make such comparisons for each business unit within their firm with comparable businesses in other firms.

Such data work adds a whole new dimension to the human resources input to the management of personnel. Now companies will be able to make judgments based not only upon how they are doing compared to how they did, and internal comparisons between similar units, but they will also be able to make judgments based upon how they are doing compared to other firms and trends in other firms.

Not all data, of course, can be compared between different businesses. One of the things that was learned in this work was the variables which must be considered in making comparisons of different general personnel data items. Size of operations and the state of the economy affect some personnel data items. The type of business is important for some data items in interbusiness personnel comparisons; and it was necessary to develop a new business classification system to deal with this issue.

There were a number of important lessons learned from this work which will benefit future activities. There was full awareness of the technical difficulties of making such general personnel comparisons. The technical difficulties, which seemed so massive when the work began, turned out to be very manageable. In fact, there were some matters of comparison far simpler in personnel data than either compensation or benefit comparisons. The items themselves, for example, were far easier to define. Quits, turnover, and salary paid are far simpler to define than job descriptions or personnel programs.

This work also suggested that critical levels of data can be identified for some items. For example, there is a rate of new hires over time which represents a critical level; hiring more than that may result in a work force insufficiently experienced to meet the goals of the firm or to work at reasonably effective levels.

An intercompany personnel data exchange can result in *profiles*; not just of what other companies are doing but also information about "best practices." Ratios of hires to promotions might be an example of one best-practices profile. Best-practices profiles provide an achievable goal. In some cases, to achieve more than the best-practices goal may involve a substantial cost with little value.

Collection and reporting of personnel data improves the excellence of the managment of personnel practices. For example, the salary increase distribution will be closer to a best-practices profile in companies that have HRIS and exchange personnel data. Managers of personnel in these organizations know that the data will be seen by top management and that their work is subject to comparison. Furthermore, when top management sees the results of data comparisons, they may take action if, in their opinion, company experiences can be improved.

HOW TO PROCEED

Some of the principal lessons learned with respect to how to proceed have already been described. Quality is the main consideration. I know companies that have two-page personnel data questionnaires. They complete them by hand at each location. It takes about half-an-hour each month at each location. But they have a uniform chart of accounts, and all the data is highly relevant and useful. They simply then combine that information at each subsequent organizational level to get overall corporate information which can be analyzed by any combination of business units. Even such a simple, hand-tabulated system has proven extremely valuable.

Keep in mind that we are in the information revolution. The availability of high-technology information processing equipment will be a force in the development of personnel data and human resources information systems. That represents both an opportunity and a danger. The information which can become available will involve all the personnel data of the company. Anyone with a terminal will have the ability to access and analyze such information on a plain English language basis. This will enhance enormously the potential contribution and effectiveness of work of all personnel professionals. But the requirements for effective use and security are serious matters.

Computers and other information technology represent a capital substitution; substituting machine power for manpower. Historically, that has been how we have increased productivity. But productivity was assured in just about all prior capital substitution activities, because the equipment purchased controlled the work of those who operated the equipment. This is not true of information equipment. With information equipment, the user of the equipment determines the work to be done. Therefore, whether the use of information technology improves productivity depends upon the skill, the intelligence, and the good judgment of those who use the equipment.

Every company now has computers, and all firms have a management information systems department that is sometimes as large as the personnel department. There are many suppliers of the most exotic type of information technology. The personnel department needs in-house professionals who understand and are conversant with all of this technology.

There has been a tendency to overbuy equipment. There has also been too much reliance on the equipment and the availability of the corporate MIS department. Companies have also erred in being inclined to buy established systems programs. Many of the preprogrammed personnel information systems that have been sold to companies were designed for many companies and, therefore, are tailored to none. Some persons in the personnel organization must be knowledgeable about MIS. Consider having such persons responsible for developing customized human resources information systems programs. You have people in your corporate MIS department who can do this work. If not, or if they are not available, hire someone from the outside. Chances are that a student at a local community college could do such work.

Human resources information systems are now an established part of personnel management and the management of personnel. Computer information technology and communications technology are the new dimension of personnel work. They are an exotic tool in the hands of personnel professionals. The capacity for improved and more effective work is breathtaking. But we haven't seen anything yet. The continued rate of improvement in the technology of information and communications continues at an accelerating rate. It is impossible to predict the technology and the capability of computers and communications systems even ten years from today. This argues also for getting on-stream now in personnel information work to maintain competitiveness and to be as effective as your competition.

Chapter 10

COMPENSATION*

For the company, compensation is a cost: and the effective management of compensation costs has already been suggested as a basic issue in the management of personnel. For the employee, compensation is income; clearly a critical issue which affects the material well-being of the worker and his or her family. Hardly ever considered is the importance of compensation to the public. In our free-choice economic system, compensation paid for different jobs in different businesses has to do with the allocation of our national treasure: our working people. So from every view, compensation is indeed a basic issue. It is also a very complicated issue; complicated mostly because there are so many technical matters and administrative considerations.

MANAGING COMPENSATION COSTS

Among the many analyses your human resources information systems could provide would be an ability to determine the effect

---

*I have written a great deal about compensation over the years even though only about one-third of my time in consulting was spent in this field. The volume of material written on compensation reflected reader interest rather than personal focus. In this chapter, however, I am only focusing on key issues, particularly as they relate to the management of personnel. For a more technical and detailed treatment of compensation, I would refer you to *Compensation*, published by AMACOM in 1981. For my own thoughts and experience with respect to management compensation I would refer you to *A Consultant's Report on Management Compensation*, published in 1984 by R.B. Keck & Company, Inc.

of compensation costs on business results under different circumstances. In time, such a system could also analyze different organizational structures, different mixes of manpower, and different managerial styles with respect to compensation costs and thereby business results. Perhaps you can't make these analyses yet, but you should know the cost impact on your firm of ± 1 percent in compensation costs on profit. You should be able to make estimates of the earnings yield from 1 percent of compensation costs alternately deployed into R&D, marketing, or improved product quality. If you can't do these things, then the first suggestion I would make is to develop the capability to do so; it is an important part of the capability to manage compensation costs.

Ten percent differences in compensation have a special relevance, because that's about what is distinguishable in survey data. The effect of 10 percent less in compensation costs on ROA would be:

- A 20 percent increase in ROA in smokestack industries.

- A 30 percent increase in ROA in high-tech industries.

- A 40 percent increase in ROA in retail chains.

Such data is "old hat," but it's a sample of the information which is available in managing compensation costs. It also illustrates that we are talking about large stakes with a very great impact on business results.

Such dollar figures should never lead management to conclude that the goal is to pay as little as possible; the less the better. You must pay sufficiently to get and retain the number and qualities of people necessary to run the business effectively. But on the other hand, paying more than is sufficient may be a costly error.

The management of compensation costs is a complex matter, so we should never be too quick to judge what might appear to be excessive pay. For openers, the management of compensation costs is complex because it involves three broad variables, each of which is complex, and it is difficult to determine what is "appropriate" or "optimum" with respect to each. These three basic variables determining compensation costs are:

- The level of job pay

- Reward for performance

- Manpower

With respect to the level of job pay (for the technical minded, this should be the salary structure midpoint), it is worth repeating that the company should pay the average unless there is a compelling business reason for doing otherwise. With respect to pay for performance, pay premiums should be equivalent to the increment of productivity reflected by higher performance. With respect to manpower, we have a very special problem.

Determining job level in the market and pay for performance are within the scope of the responsibilities of the compensation professional, and they can do work to support the achievement of such goals. Manpower control is rarely the accountability of the compensation professional. Accountability for manpower may be in various places. Frequently it's in the controller's department; sometimes it isn't assigned anywhere. Here we see an example of the essential interrelationship of each facet of personnel to every other. Manpower controls substantially affect the management of compensation costs but they are not a part of the direct accountability of the compensation department. Compensation costs are excessive in many firms because of surplus manpower.

COMPETITIVE PAY

There are only five practical differences in the level of the competitiveness of pay for jobs. One of these is to pay at statistical average. The second competitive practice is to pay above average; about 10 percent above statistical average. Another is to pay high; about 20 percent above average. Companies may pay below average; a full 10 percent below statistical average. Under very unusual circumstances a company may pay low; 20 percent below average.

A company gains little advantage in the marketplace by having salaries 10 percent above average, and it is not seriously disadvantaged in the marketplace if salaries are 10 percent below average. This assumes, of course, that the company has sound recruiting practices.

You can prove statistically that you are truly competitive if you pay salaries for jobs which are market average, employ the correct recruiting practices, and do vertical recruiting. Thus all the company's objectives are achieved by paying market average for jobs. To pay more, unless there is a substantial business reason, would be superfluous and a questionable use of company monies. To pay less than average is of questionable fairness to people who work in the firm and can cause problems for your firm.

A firm should have substantial business reasons for paying above or below average. For example, a company might pay above average or high salaries because they have no bonus plan or no long-term income plan; because they are particularly transactional in the marketplace for a given group of jobs; or because there are conditions which make employment in their firm unattractive (such as their location). A company may set some salaries below average if it is experiencing severe business difficulties or if it has highly attractive conditions of work.

PRICING JOBS

Qualified compensation people know how to price jobs. They are very good at it. Let them do their job.

There is plenty of survey data available for these compensation professionals to do that job. Much of it is good data; and the qualified compensation professional knows the data that is not good. There will be a great deal more market pay data available as we move into the era of information technology.

Not all survey data is of equal quality. There are two important variables. The first is who does the surveying. The second is what methods are used.

Some organizations that conduct surveys do a very high-quality job. Their work results in survey data which is accurate ±5 to 10 percent. That's as good as you'll ever get. It is plenty good enough to determine "market pay" for jobs in your company. The survey work of some other firms is terrible; it's hard to believe how bad they are.

The survey method used is also important. My opinion is that job matching, where there are actual comparisons of jobs by visits, meetings, or telephone conversations, is by far the best. Mailed surveys that are uncontrolled are worthless. Information-based surveys are good enough and cost very little. Surveys based upon job evaluation points, in my opinion, are not good enough. I have always had grave doubts about pricing jobs by regression analysis. However, some compensation professionals who I respect very highly think it a sound process; so I must be wrong about this.

In addition to surveys, I have urged companies to use their employment experience in order to price jobs in the market. The number of people hired each year by many firms equals 10 percent of their work force. In the process of employment they see many candidates for each job opening; and have an opportunity to learn about the job of each applicant as well as an opportunity to evaluate the person. They can match that person's current job against jobs within their own company until they make the "best match." This is real market information; utilization of this information is being truly "market sensitive."

Market activity is even a better way of learning about market pay than the data may suggest. Typically, 50 percent of a firm's employment experience is focused on 5 percent of its jobs. It has that employment experience in many of the same jobs year after year. A firm also tends to lose people from these same jobs; and with exit interviewing it can also get information about jobs people go to and the money they are paid. The sample of companies being "surveyed" by this employment experience is not artificial; based, for example, on those who are willing to participate in a survey or the clients of a surveyor. These companies are your real labor market competition.

Companies should have a formal system for recording and reporting their market experience. It is a valid method of market-pricing jobs. To do this, the employment people would simply have to identify the job in your firm most like the job held by the applicants (whether hired or not) and record the actual pay they received when they applied. Employment people would require only a moderate amount of training to do this work. In many ways, you would find that it was a better monitoring system of the marketplace than all the surveys you now participate in. Furthermore, the employment market-pricing process will cost very little.

THE SIBSON JOB EVALUATION METHOD

I said before that traditional job evaluation *programs* were increasingly less useful and not usable for many jobs. I think I can prove this to any reasonable and impartial person; and I have done so on a number of occasions. Nevertheless, there are special circumstances when companies might use a job evaluation program anyway. For instance, they may use it as a disciplinary measure to force managers to do better job grading. Such actions are, of course, strong medicine; they should only be used when essential; and they should be temporary measures.

However, we must have job level information about jobs that cannot be priced directly in the marketplace. Such "nonbenchmarked jobs" must also be graded in the salary structure to have an orderly pay administration system and in order to have a proxy measure of competitiveness. I think the Sibson Job Evaluation Method is by far the most effective and least costly method of classifying nonbenchmarked jobs; those that cannot be priced directly in the marketplace.

This method, which is a *system* rather than a *program*, has three distinct elements. These are:

- Benchmarking
- A job grading system for nonbenchmark jobs
- Monitoring

Benchmarking assigns jobs that can be priced by surveying or from monitoring employment experience into salary grades. You take the market salary that has been determined and put the job in the grade where the midpoint is closest to the market data. It's as simple as that. It is the responsibility of the corporate compensation department to do benchmarking, although they may have others in the organization assisting them.

You will find that between 5 and 15 percent of all the jobs in your company can be priced through benchmarking. This is the anchor of the Sibson Job Evaluation Method. When jobs have been assigned a grade by benchmarking, that assignment of grade cannot be changed by anyone in the organization. Benchmarking reflects the market, and if company policy is to position jobs against the market then no manager, regardless of his rank or his reasons, may change that policy and therefore those results.

It is the job of each manager of personnel to determine the appropriate grade for all other jobs; the "nonbenchmarked" jobs. This is the second element of the Sibson Job Evaluation Method. It is the manager of personnel who determines the proper grade for nonbenchmarked jobs.

Nonbenchmarked jobs are, by definition, those that cannot be priced in the marketplace. Therefore, someone must make a judgment as to the proper grade for those jobs. Under the Sibson Job Evaluation Method, that is the job of the manager of personnel because the manager of personnel knows the jobs best and is responsible for those jobs and the people who work in those jobs.

There are many ways in which the manager of personnel could discharge his responsibility for grading nonbenchmarked jobs. There is, however, one critical requirement. The manager of personnel, regardless of how else he may grade the nonbench-marked jobs, must make decisions by comparing his nonbench-marked jobs against all relevant benchmarked jobs (and this includes benchmarked jobs in his group and those not in his group).

Here is the method that I suggest the manager of personnel use. The personnel generalist who supports the manager of personnel would make up white three-by-five-inch cards for each of the nonbenchmarked jobs reporting to the manager of personnel. The personnel generalist would also make up blue three-by-five-inch cards for all benchmarked jobs that are relevant for comparison with any of the nonbenchmarked jobs under the responsibility of the manager of personnel.

The manager of personnel then ranks the jobs: comparing each nonbenchmarked job with benchmarked jobs and other non-benchmarked jobs. The personnel generalist assists him in this process; asking questions and making suggestions.

Personally, I like to use four factors and have quite conventional degrees and point weightings for the process. The factors I use are: responsibility, knowledge, skill, and conditions. Under this approach, you get the manager of personnel to rank each position by each factor. I like this because I find that managers of personnel can do ranking better by factors. Then the personnel generalist adds up the points for all jobs and shows the manager of personnel the resulting rankings. When the manager of personnel sees the results, he will reconsider some of the rankings.

Note that there are no job descriptions used in this process. The manager of personnel knows the jobs so he doesn't need them. Of course, if there are descriptions prepared for some other reason, bring them along. But you will find the manager of personnel won't refer to them.

This whole process can be done carefully and thoughtfully in a very short period of time. Grading will rarely take more than one hour for each 20 jobs. And there are only two people involved: the manager of personnel and the personnel generalist; unless, of course, the manager of personnel also brings directors of work into the meeting and has them participate in the process. What this means is that, even in a large firm with 20,000 employees, there is a total of 2,000 man hours per year spent on job grading; and the company doesn't have to hire consultants to be involved in any of this work.

The results of the job grading of each of the managers of personnel is recorded and fed into the computer and the human resources information system. This information is available for the monitoring and review of the corporate compensation group.

The monitoring by the corporate compensation group is the third element of the Sibson Job Evaluation Method. It is monitoring; personnel auditing. The corporate compensation department has all of these gradings available, and it can review the judgments of every manager. The method I urge them to use is "computer-aided ranking." In effect, you simply develop a systems program which can call up various types of comparisons; by job, by organization, by function, etc. All types of comparisons can be called up electronically; dozens of them in one hour. This is quality management; it is a personnel audit. By this method, the corporate compensation department can identify any potential bias or errors before they become serious problems.

FREE CHOICE

You may call our economic system "capitalist," but so much capital is provided by the government or institutional investors that many markets which exist today don't really square with the definition of capitalism you read in economics books. You may want to call our economic system "free enterprise," but private companies are so regulated that "free" hardly seems to fit; and I fear that the conduct of some firms is not described well by the word "enterprise." "Capitalism" and "free enterprise" were always the visible characteristics of our economic system anyway. The essence of that system has always been FREE CHOICE.*

Employers have free choice as to whom they hire and at what pay. If firms are managed by intelligent and prudent business persons, they will hire the most suitable candidates who will become the most effective workers.

The choices of employers are not completely free.** Legislation has limited choices in a number of ways to achieve social goals. To the extent that these limitations result in the employment of less effective workers and lower productivity, the politicians, consciously or not, have valued their social purpose above the material well-being of the American people.

When pay for jobs is not based on the market, then pay is regulated. Regulated pay causes improper allocation of our nation's talent. This is what makes the proper management of compensation of national importance.

It is free choice, which makes the maintenance of job rates at market average the correct thing for a firm to do unless there

---

*"The Free-Choice Economic System" is a chapter in *Common Sense Answers*. How the free-choice system affects the management of compensation is the sole focus here.

**Employees also have free choice in labor markets. Legislators have not yet directly limited employee choices.

are compelling business reasons for doing otherwise. To pay job rates above market is a misuse of company funds. Of course, those who receive more are better off; but at the expense of other workers who must pay higher prices for the goods and services provided by those favored by regulated pay. Favoring some by higher than market pay penalizes others also, because equally qualified persons who would choose to work at market pay are not permitted to do so. Of course, individual persons who work in a superior manner should get more than market pay. But you don't reward some high-performing person by paying more to everyone. You reward people for their performance by your performance award system.

PERFORMANCE REWARD SYSTEMS IN BUSINESS

Business has done a good job of providing financial rewards for employees for more effective work. There is no doubt that this accomplishment by business has contributed considerably to the vitality of our business system and the success of businesses in creating jobs and wealth. However, in the management of personnel it is important to understand what these pay reward systems are and the importance of each of them.

First, we know that rewards are both monetary and non-monetary. We must never underestimate the importance of non-financial "rewards." The degree to which employees find their work fulfilling and the degree to which they have the skills and talent to do that work well are rewards. Qualities of leadership in management, the working environment, and the degree to which employees have the proper facilities for doing their work are all vital to effective work and represent a form of reward. Also, doing good work is its own reward.

As far as financial rewards are concerned, it is extremely important never to forget that there are three distinctly different types of financial reward systems in business. These are merit salary increase systems, incentive pay and promotions. Each of these is identified, with comments, in *Exhibit 10-1*.

Throughout business, for all employees, promotion is by far the most important financial element of reward, affecting the

Exhibit 10-1

FINANCIAL REWARDS SYSTEMS IN BUSINESS

Form of Reward
(Comments relate to extent and importance of reward system)

Type of Work	Merit Salary	Incentive Pay	Promotion
Executive and Senior Management	"Merit salary" not applicable. Differences in salary make small differences in total pay.	Bonus, long-term income, and special benefits represent *the* rewards system.	Applies to few.
Middle-Level	Extremely important for "career-peaked" employees.	Applies to few: rewards are moderate.	Most important reward system for majority.
Operations	Mixed: many employees on flat rate; many others receive increases automatically with time.	Only one of five persons covered by incentive plan, but for some, rewards are substantial.	Most important reward system for majority.

most people and involving the most dollars of increased compensation for individuals. Incentive pay is the second most important element of reward, both in terms of the number of people meaningfully affected and the dollars involved. Merit salary increases, while important, are third in importance in business financial reward systems.

Many operations-level employees are paid a single fixed rate or get increases automatically with time. Merit increase plans have not worked well historically in operations-level jobs. There have been problems with supervisors' judgments of "merit"; particularly where output and quality are, at least in part, measurable. Also, the spread in pay from "standard" to "maximum" is rather small at these levels because of modest performance spread.

The establishment of the job of manager of personnel will be a big step forward in assuring proper judgments about performance. So will improved performance appraisal systems. So far as the amount of pay premiums for more effective work, be sure your ranges are sufficient, particularly in view of increased technology even in many operations-level jobs. Look also at what the dollar differences mean before concluding that they are insufficient; at the operations level, small dollar differences materially affect the *cost of living*, not just the style of living.

For some factory workers, production incentive plans are important rewards. Less than one-third of all operations workers in this country are now covered by such pay plans. Such plans need to be reviewed constantly; primarily because of a tendency for performance standards to erode.

There are some operations-level workers who never get a promotion; entering the labor market in the lowest unskilled job category and remaining at that work level throughout their careers. There is no promotion incentive pay for them. But nine of ten production workers and office workers get at least one promotion in their working lives. For them, promotion is significant, in that their pay is improved more by promotion than either incentive pay plans or merit salary programs.

Among middle-level people, promotion is by far the number one financial reward. At any given point in time in a company, four of five middle-level people still have the potential for at least one future promotion. Almost all middle-level people receive at least three promotions during their careers, so promotions affect the most people and involve the most dollars.

Incentive pay plans cover relatively few middle-level people. The reward systems which exist do not involve much money and they are highly discretionary. Almost all middle-level people are salaried and in jobs where there is a salary range to be paid; and therefore, potentially, they should be the beneficiaries of merit salary increase programs. Merit salary differences between standard or acceptable levels and outstanding work can and should be significant. This is particularly true of high-performing, middle-level people who have career peaked.

In my opinion, there is a great need and opportunity to develop effective incentive pay plans for groups of middle-level workers. It's one subject that is on my developmental project list. So far as merit salary increase programs are concerned, they should be very effective at middle levels. If you have any doubts about this in your firm, make it a high priority item for review.

Promotional opportunities are rare among executives and senior managers; many of them have career peaked. Salary increases based upon "merit" are not generally a part of salary practices for high-level managers. Therefore, all of the reward systems for their jobs are in the form of incentive pay. For people who reach senior management levels, income from incentive pay systems can exceed salary.

Essentially, in pay increase administration as in pay level determination, it must be the manager of personnel who has the authority and the responsibility to make decisions. He may receive many guidelines and much support in this work. Compensation professionals have developed many of these guidelines. We have erred, perhaps, in trying to apply these guidelines as *programs*, in a uniform manner without consideration of the individuals or the circumstances.

SOME KEY PAY ISSUES

I have written a great deal about management pay during the past year. There was *A Consultant's Report on Management Compensation*. The fall issue of *The Sibson Report* contained the 20th

Annual Management Compensation Study; and the whole report was devoted to that study. There is much to be said about management pay; but I think that in those two publications I have said basically what I have to say. Therefore, in this book, I have just a few comments to make.

The chief executive officer in a business is the captain of that ship. By law and as a practical necessity, the CEO is one person who is essentially *unmanaged*; and that sometimes applies also to a few very close associate executives. There can only be one captain: don't expect the board to manage.

But, like the captain of the ship, the CEO has such great authority because the responsibility is great; responsibility for the welfare of stakeholders and for achieving the public mission of the firm. The CEO should be monitored very closely to ensure that he is properly discharging his responsibilities to the stakeholders, and that includes employee partners. The board should do that monitoring. One of the specific activities which the board must perform is with respect to the pay of the chief executive officer and other key executive officers. They must act with independence in this work; and of course they must be qualified to do the work.

In *A Consultant's Report on Management Compensation*, I outlined specific things which, in my opinion, the board should do with respect to executive pay. There are only a few, and they have been summarized in a four-page report. This summary has been sent to hundreds of interested people; and we will send a complimentary copy to anyone who requests it. Very few boards now do the sorts of things I have recommended and which I think are essential. This is *the* critical problem of the management of executive pay.

Here are some critical issues with respect to the management of middle-level compensation. First, we need to do a better job of pricing. I think the techniques for doing so are available; and one of them is pricing by employment experience.

I think the opportunity for the effective management of management pay at the middle levels can only be achieved and realized through delegative management. For the management of middle-level pay, the managers of personnel are very high-level persons; supported by experienced personnel persons.

While we have in business done a good job of rewarding through promotions, it is such a vital element of management pay at the middle levels that I think it needs constant monitoring and nurturing. This essentially is outside the scope of the compensation professional; involving such activities as career pathing and management development.

At operations levels (i.e., in the factory and in the office), there are some serious problems. These are not just technical compensation problems. They are basic substantive problems of management. They seriously affect the level of productivity.

Problem number one is that the real earnings of many operations-level people have been down-trending for the past ten years. This obviously creates a financial burden, and it must reduce morale and the inclination to do one's best. Here is my advice to companies with respect to the problem of declining real earnings of operations-level workers:

- First, communicate to employees about real earnings, and tell them the truth. Give your employees the facts about the real earnings of American workers generally and exactly what is happening to the real pay of people in your firm.

- As a matter of basic company policy, commit your firm to keep wages of *jobs* up with market inflation, regardless of the impact on profitability. Be careful to emphasize to employees that it is not your intention to try to match increases in the Consumer Price Index, but rather to match increases in job pay with the market.

- Develop a productivity improvement program for your firm and enlist your employees' support. Set out to increase employee productivity through more effective employee work. Point out that as productivity improves so will business results. Job opportunities will be created, and there will be more increases both because of promotion and because of the operation of your merit pay increase program. Also, as business results improve, more money will go into profit-sharing plans for the benefit of employees. That's another way to raise pay to match or exceed inflation.

- Finally, give constant attention to your own promotion from within programs and to your merit salary increase program.

Another serious issue is that more than 20 percent of the full-time people working in our companies have annual incomes from their jobs which are below the government's published poverty threshold; which was $9,852 when this book was being written. Now the real problem is that the government's figure is incorrect; errors were made when the study was conducted in 1964, and they have been compounded for 20 years by improper indexing. Actually, the poverty threshold published by the government is about 25 percent higher than it should be. The real average poverty threshold for a family of four is about $7,500.

Working people, however, don't know about these statistics. Political leaders take advantage of this and preach over and over about the fact that 35 million people live in poverty; and, of course, they will correct all of that if they are elected. Your people see that $9,852 figures in the press, and if their annual income is less than that, they think that they have been working all year to earn a level of income which leaves them in poverty.

Someday, I hope a media source will pick up this story and then the politicians will be embarrassed into setting the correct poverty threshold number. At that point, I would certainly be the first to suggest that we get to where we should be by future containment of increases in the poverty threshold rather than a cut.

A third really serious problem of pay for operations workers which affects the management of personnel is that of "net pay." Net pay is the money received after work expenses and after taxes. A salary of $240 per week ($6 per hour) may sound pretty good; $12,000 per year. But federal, state, and local taxes take about $3,000. The cost of work (and particularly the cost of transportation to and from work) may cost another $1,000. That means that net pay is $8,000 per year; a little over $150 per week; less than $4 per hour. Even the worker who earns the national average of about $22,000 per year ($10 per hour) has a net pay of less than $14,000; a little more than $250 per week; less than $7 per hour.

There is very little a company can do about this problem.

Perhaps you could improve the situation through your recruiting (getting people closer to your work places) or through car pools and other types of actions. But all of these will have a minimal effect, and the company can't do anything about taxes.

Chapter 11

BENEFIT COST CONTAINMENT

An important part of managing compensation costs involves the management of benefits costs. Benefits are simply another form of compensation. The total value of benefits, as a percentage of salary, ranges from 20 to 40 percent. Benefit cost containment involves some very special problems.

PROBLEM NUMBER ONE: HEALTH INSURANCE

The problem of cost containment of health insurance could not be better said than it was in one of the quarterly reports written by and for participants of our fall personnel management conference:

A subject which received only cursory discussion during our October conference and yet remains as one of the most important issues in personnel management today is that of managing health care costs. A recent study projected that if premium costs continue to increase at 25 percent per year and wages increase by 8 percent annually, medical insurance will exceed payroll costs by the year 2001.

We have created a health care system in our country where the purchaser (employer) and the consumer (employee) have little to say about what is purchased, its price, quantity or quality. These decisions are made by the providers (doctors and hospitals) who are also the recipients of the payments; a truly unique business system.

You could quarrel with the details of this projection. If you did, you would simply arrive at a different date when the levels of benefit costs would become intolerable. The point of intolerability will come long before benefit costs equal pay costs. As long as health care costs increase at a rate higher than pay costs, we will inevitably reach the point of intolerability in the level of health costs, and we will be there very soon.

The containment of health care costs has become a high-priority item in just about every company. Because of this, companies have adopted a variety of actions to contain the increase in health care costs. These include some form of policing or monitoring; some technical actions; and having employees pay a part of (or an increasing part of) the health care costs.

Policing may sound like too harsh a word, but the fact of the matter is that, when they look closely, companies are finding that there are some abuses of health care benefits. It's not so much a matter of cheating or fraud. Policing involves discouraging frivolous claims or health care (and, therefore, health care costs) which are more cosmetic than therapeutic.

If policing is to be effective and positive, it must occur mostly by the actions of the managers of personnel assisted by personnel generalists. At this level in the organization, there can be a direct conversation; assuring proper benefit payments but also making sure that people themselves recognize the need for benefit cost containment and why it is important to all employees. If this is done effectively, companies may find that their employees, by the nature of their reactions and conversations with other employees, are part of the cost containment effort.

Some of this requires effective communications. Clearly, part of the problem of benefit cost containment is the perception by many that the collection of benefits, however frivolous or cosmetic, doesn't cost anything. It is not unnatural for people covered by insured benefits to think that the company has already paid for the benefits and so they're merely getting what they are entitled to and what has already been paid for; and, in fact, the insurance company is paying anyway. If employees understand that the company's costs are determined by their benefit claim experience, then we may find that employee partners become a part of a benefit cost containment effort.

Companies have also initiated technical actions; many quite

complicated and clearly an area for the benefit specialist. There are, for example, some actuarial assumptions in benefit plans that are suspect. Brokers' fees may properly be renegotiated. Companies may do a better job of shopping around for the best buy in employee benefit packages. My advice to companies would be to let the specialist loose on this subject. There is a clear need, and there has been enough evidence that actions can result in better containment of benefit costs.

Many firms have always had the policy of having employees pay a part of every benefit. The thinking is that employees then will always be mindful of the fact that they have the benefits and that there is a cost associated with all of them. On the other hand, employee contributions are tax inefficient. Increasingly, companies are concluding, as a matter of cost containment alone, that even token employee contributions to health care costs contribute importantly to benefit cost containment.

Personally, I prefer an approach where the company pays the full cost of very basic health insurance for the employee only. Then different supplemental health care plans would be available on a contributive basis: and the percentage of employee contributions could vary between these plans from nominal contributions to 100 percent.

There are an increasing number of basic matters with respect to the management of personnel and the productivity of the work force which are beyond the control of any single employer. Some require group action; and there are many items of group action which could be undertaken within the structure of existing law. Examples would be shared personnel research and group personnel data exchanges. There are other matters which vitally affect the management of personnel which all companies, collectively, can do little about. The containment of health costs is one of these issues.

It is, as a matter of fact, instructive that companies only talk about "cost containment": slowing down the rate of increase in health costs. Rarely do they talk about cost control or cost reduction in the area of health costs. All the company actions combined can, at best, contain the increase in health care costs. But there is also hope for cost reduction in health care; but reductions in health care costs are in the hands of the politicians.

A decision must be made about the level of health care which

142

will be provided and the basis of availability. One reason why health costs have been escalating is because the quality of health care has improved very greatly and, thanks partially to company health insurance benefits, the best medical care is being extended to more and more people. That's progress; but it's also at the heart of the problem of health care costs.

If every person in this country were granted the best medical care possible and we continued improvement in the quality of health care, medical costs could theoretically exceed the national income some day. At some time, therefore, there must be a political decision to either restrain advances in medicine or somehow restrict the availability of health care services.

It is not likely that the government or the politicians will, in fact, restrain advances in medical research primarily because so much of this work is outside the control of the government. Inevitably, therefore, the politicians must face up to the issue of restricting in some way the delivery of the health care services which are available. Historically, this had been done on the basis of ability to pay. If that's not acceptable, then there must be some other system devised by the politicians to allocate health care services.

A second major element of health care costs in the hands of the legislators involves medical malpractice; which really means medical mistakes. Laws and court decisions involving medical mistakes cost the working men and women in this country in two ways. First, mistake insurance (erroneously called malpractice insurance) is paid for by the users; doctors pass it on in their fees. Second, medical bills are bloated by many tests and procedures designed only to avoid legal suits. Changing current mistake insurance to true malpractice insurance would *reduce* medical costs in this country by at least 10 percent.

A third issue in health cost control involves the doctors. More than half of all the services performed by doctors could be provided by registered nurses and paramedics if it were legally possible for them to do so. Actually, they are now doing this in the armed services and in some sections of the country where doctors won't work because they can't earn enough money. Use of licensed paramedics would reduce medical costs by at least another 10 percent.

Politicians could, therefore, reduce health care costs without

143

any diminution in health care protection by at least 20 percent. They won't do it.

PROBLEM NUMBER TWO: RETIREMENT BENEFITS

While most of the current attention is focused on health costs, pensions are also a big problem. Retirement costs are also excessive and escalating. There will very likely be further legal changes affecting private pension plans which could increase the cost of retirement benefits to a level of intolerability. Furthermore, our population is aging, largely because of better health care, and that's adding to the problem of retirement benefit cost containment.

Social Security retirement benefits cost too much now, and they will increase again before very long. It's no secret that the whole Social Security program is a mess, and it can't be patched anymore. But that whole subject is another political problem; and current legislators won't really deal with the problems, viewing them as a "get elected problem for someone in the future." What all that suggests to companies is that they had best rethink their retirement programs. They had best rely less on Social Security payments and company retirement plans when they think about retirement income for employees in their own firm.

There has been a three-tiered philosophy of retirement income in this country since the 1930s. Social Security was to be available for all workers; and was designed to provide income at retirement to provide for minimum living standards (i.e., a poverty threshold for retired persons). The second tier was to come from company retirement programs. Company retirement benefits, when combined with Social Security benefits, were designed to be sufficient to provide an income at retirement sufficient for living in decency and comfort. Companies aimed at combined benefits of about 50 percent of salary at the time of retirement from their company retirement programs and Social Security. Then it was thought that the workers themselves, through their savings, would add whatever income was necessary to achieve the style of living in retirement they chose and could afford.

144

All three elements of this three-tiered retirement philosophy are in trouble. Social Security problems have been greatly publicized and need no further comment here. It's also common knowledge that, particularly among our young people, it is increasingly difficult to save; many find it impossible even to acquire the capital to make their first home purchase. Private retirement plans are also in very deep trouble.

Company retirement programs involve major risks and open-ended costs. Potentially, these increased costs could have a major impact on the company's profits and its ability to succeed or survive. Some types of retirement plans face greater risks and far greater open-ended costs than others; but all are vulnerable.

For example, the ten-year vesting requirement of ERISA is a problem. The ten-year vesting increased unfunded liabilities of pensions substantially in most firms. However, ten-year vesting is not likely to be the end. Ultimately, we will likely have full portability. There is logic and fairness in full portability, but this would increase enormously the unfunded liability of any pension plan.

There is also increased pressure to index retirement benefits of those who have already retired and to start indexing all benefits for people who will retire. There is clearly a real need to do something because of the impact of inflation on fixed pension benefits. Workers who retire with a company pension equal to 50 percent of their salary at the time of retirement (and very few are that fortunate) would find that, if we experience future rates of inflation consistent with those which have existed over the past ten years, their retirement income will fall to about one-third that amount, if they have average life expectancy after retirement.*

Some suggest indexing, but I think that is a very poor answer which would involve enormous costs for the company.** The combination of shorter vesting or full portability and indexing

---

*A worker retiring with a $12,000 company pension today would, in real dollars, be receiving less than $4,000 in the year 2000.
**There are also technical problems with indexing; indexing of retirement benefits represents an open-ended claim on the income of future workers; and, with indexing, retired persons would logically favor inflation.

would be so great that many companies would simply be forced to terminate existing retirement plans.

Companies that tie pension benefits to final years' pay have a very special risk. Under these plans, pension costs would double each ten years if current rates of inflation continue.

Finally, companies face unknowns. Who knows what kind of additional regulatory requirements, rules and regulations, changed tax treatment, or other government initiatives might reduce even more the value of company retirement benefit programs or increase their cost even more.

Companies still have compelling reasons for providing continued income for employees who become too old to work; just as they have a business need to provide funds to support employees who incur health problems. But to meet those clear business needs and compelling employee relations objectives, companies will have to rethink their retirement income strategies. The three-tiered retirement philosophy still has great logic and merit, but how it is achieved must change. Essentially, companies must move away from traditional retirement programs (and particularly fixed benefit programs) and emphasize more employee estate-building plans based partially on profit sharing.

PROBLEM NUMBER THREE: "EVERYBENEFIT"

There are times when you would think that benefit specialists are out to develop company programs to protect employees from every possible risk: "everybenefit" programs. Benefits started out to provide partial retirement income, protection from major health risks, and a cushion of death benefits. But we are well on our way in business to providing fully insured protection against every risk; and there are those in benefits work who would get companies to provide "everybenefit," completely at company expense.

Now there are also "individualized benefits." These are designed to give employees choices so that they can pick that benefit coverage which meets their needs the best. The basic idea certainly has great merit. But it also involves great difficulty with the Internal Revenue Service and, I fear, may involve major problems in the future. Individualized benefits also involve difficult choices for employees. How can an employee really know whether to choose more health insurance or life insurance if he doesn't know whether he is going to get sick or die? But however laudable the idea of individualized benefits may be, they represent another movement toward "everybenefit."

You can't really be against better family insured protection, but, unfortunately, all of these things cost money. They involve the issue of benefit cost containment. It's money that goes to "everybenefit" instead of pay. Money itself is the ultimate flexible benefit.

These company benefits are cost efficient only because they are tax sheltered. But this means that your employees pay for some of their benefits and other employees pay the rest of their benefits. But then other employees in other companies have "everybenefit," and then your employees pay some of the costs of those benefits.

So employees pay. Working men and women pay all the bills: but our society is getting very tricky about making it seem like we pay less than we really do. That's good politics but very poor economics. A way of really achieving benefit cost containment is to let those who are paying know exactly what they are paying, what they are paying for, and who the beneficiaries are.*

PROBLEM NUMBER FOUR:
SPECIAL BENEFITS FOR EXECUTIVES

I have dealt enough in *A Consultant's Report on Management Compensation* with special benefits for executives. There are many of them. The cost of some is not great, but the cost of all, when combined, is substantial. In my mind, equally important is the fact that the level of resentment by working people toward these special benefits for those who can afford them the most is

---

*In *Common Sense Answers* I ask, "Why are there any company deductions for benefit plans at all?" My answer in this case is that company payments for benefits should be treated like pay: a tax deduction for the company and taxable income for employees; no tax sheltered income at all for anyone.

becoming intense. This makes the special benefits for executives a problem with respect to the management of personnel.

In summary, I made four recommendations:

- Identify every time of special benefit or perquisite for executives.

- Identify the business purpose served by each of them.

- Estimate the cost of each one.

- Have the board take a more hands-on responsibility for such benefits for executives.

The first three of these recommendations seemed to be prudent management; the fourth seemed logical. *A Consultant's Report on Management Compensation* has only been published for one year now, but I see no evidence that these recommendations have received serious consideration.

I still think these recommendations with respect to special benefits for executives have merit. I think they are important in the management of compensation. I think they are also important with respect to the effective management of personnel if, indeed, we are to have equivalency of treatment of all who work in the firm and an employee-partner philosophy throughout the organization.

There is one other issue that has been raised recently. It is an issue which should be of great concern; primarily, I think, because there are some legal experts who think it is an inevitable event. Keep in mind that most special benefits for executives are "nonqualified." That means that amounts of money expended for these special benefits for executives are not deductible as a business expense for tax purposes at the time of expenditure. This raises the question of whether such expenditures, at least when made, are legitimate business expenses. This, in turn, may raise the legal question of whether companies are expending stockholder money for purposes which are not legitimate business matters; and that could lead to legal suits.

Chapter 12

ORGANIZATIONAL STRUCTURING

Correct organizational structuring is an important part of the effective management of personnel. Organization has to do with how work is done within a firm; identifying, if not describing, basic responsibility areas, principal working relationships, and those who supervise. These are illustrative of factors that are influenced by the organizational structure of a firm, and this, in turn, impacts the effectiveness of work.

Prior to the 1960s, organizational work was a discipline of business, and companies applied organizational structuring rules in an affirmative way to improve productivity and ultimately to enhance business results. Principles and rules for organization existed which were thought to have merit and which were very broadly applied, such as span of control and one man/one boss. There were organization experts, such as Ernest Dale, who specialized in this area and built reputations from this work.

Starting in the early 1960s, these organizational rules rapidly became less effective and unusable. Experience has proven that some of them were incorrect. Mostly, however, it was the increased technology of work and the diversity of work that obsoleted the rules of organization which had served business rather well.

By the early 1970s, the rules and principles of organization were gone. This important discipline of management was no longer practiced, because the rules that had been used were no longer valid. Organization of business then fell into disarray; contributing substantially, I think, to declining productivity.

Then some business executives and personnel professionals saw the problems of organization and had no rules and principles to guide them. In the absence of rules, they worked harder and applied good judgment. From a number of such common-sense experiences emerged a new understanding about effective organizational structuring of enterprises today. Reflection on some success cases identified some new guidelines. During the past three years, primarily from the experience of dozens of cases, considerable effort has been devoted to identifying new organizational guidelines and knowledge as to where and how to apply them.

These new organizational tools are called guidelines rather than principles or rules, because they represent guides to organizational thinking rather than rules to be rigidly applied. In former years, organizational work involved mastering the principles and rules of organization and then bending and shaping the organization to fit these principles. Organization work today involves identifying organizational problems and then using the guidelines to think through and make judgments about proper organization structures.

A considerable number of such organizational guidelines have been identified. Specifics of how to apply them and under what circumstances are at various stages of development. Therefore, the usability of each guideline not only varies from company to company but is in different degrees of development. All, however, have some usability. Here are the 36 guidelines which have resulted from work in this area. They are not all separate and distinct, but each has its special point.

A number of these guidelines deal with the basic issues of organizational structuring. These include:

1. Use multiple approaches toward organization.
2. Focus work by top executives on strategic issues.
3. Concentrate on critical success areas.
4. Organize by business areas.
5. Focus organization outward.
6. Design organization for the effective management of people.
7. Consider primarily the flow of work and the basic efficiency of work at lower levels.
8. Where necessary, apply reconciliation.

9. Assign responsibility for knowledge in organizational work.
10. Conduct special purpose projects.
11. Gear the company to quick reaction.

A number of other guidelines would be more in the category of process or mechanics:

12. The delegative method of management applies.
13. Essential responsibility for organizational work must rest with the managers of personnel.
14. Span of management has replaced span of control.
15. Most organizational work is transactional; reacting to needs.
16. The loose/tight concepts of management apply to organization.
17. Matrix organizations are a standard part of modern organization.
18. Much of the work is performed by project groups.
19. Networking is a part of organization.
20. The concept of grouping of functions is important.
21. Organizations should be reported by picturing as well as traditional boxing.
22. Avoid major organizational projects.

Some of these guidelines are more in the category of tactics or ideas for organizational work:

23. Recognize that much of organization is temporary, by design.
24. Simulate smallness wherever possible.
25. Neutralize the bureaucracy of bigness.
26. Insulate business operations from noncontributory work.
27. Use manpower ratios wherever possible.
28. Recognize the need for organizational fluidity.
29. Utilize information technology and communications technology in organizational work.
30. Determine the cost of organizational changes.
31. Apply the "compelling need principle."
32. Avoid standing committees of all types.
33. Conduct practical research and experimentation with respect to organization.

34. Avoid redundancy in organization.
35. Do organizational work only for organizational purposes.
36. Don't copy organizations of other companies.

Multiple Approaches: There are four different directions in organizational work which require you to think in terms of multiple organization approaches. The four directions are:

- Organize from the top down, considering basic executive management activities, the skills of incumbents, and the strategic opportunities of the firm.

- Organize from the bottom up, considering flow of work and efficiency.

- Organize outward, focusing toward customers.

- Organize also for the basic purpose of managing people effectively.

Focus at the Top: Executive management should basically be focusing their attention on critical problems and the strategic objectives of the firm. Organization at the top must also necessarily reflect the interests and special skills of each of the principal executives of the firm, whether logical or not. Organization of a large company at the top should be perceived more as an organization of the work among partners rather than the traditional bureaucratic and structured work relationships typical of big corporations in the past.

Critical Success Areas: In all businesses there are critical activities; critical to the survival or the success of the business. For example, in some packaged food businesses, quality control is critical; in pharmaceuticals, it's research. Organization of the firm should reflect these critical success areas. Oversimplistically, quality control should report directly to the chief executive officer in a packaged food business.

Organize by Businesses: The most critical guideline of organization today is that the firm should be organized below the level of executive management, based upon the business areas of the firm. Addressing the question, "What business are we in?" is a much practiced pastime in management today. Answer the question practically. For most companies, the answer will be that we are in a number of businesses; and each of them should be a business area with complete resources, reporting directly to executive management.

Never isolate the businesses from the CEO. Normally, the head of each business should report directly to the CEO.

If you have too many businesses for each of them to report to the chief executive officer, then establish operating companies, each with its own chief operating officer or whatever you want to call him. These should become semiautonomous operating companies, where the clustering of businesses is basically made on the grounds of similar economic and operating characteristics and commonality of customers.

Below the business level, establish as many units for management and control purposes as possible. In most businesses there will be three levels of units: divisions; profit centers; and operating units.

Focus Outward: To the maximum extent possible, design the organization so that an individual's natural tendency is to look outward rather than inward. Ultimately, the outward look should be to the customers who are served. The tendency in big business is to look inward and to deal with itself; but the real world of business is pointed toward customers and customers' needs.

In most instances, having a sales department is not enough. Product development, manufacturing, and at least components of finance and personnel should focus toward customers and customers' needs.

Organize to Manage People: The principles of the manager of personnel have already been described. Design the organization to establish managers of personnel throughout the organization.

Recognize also in this work that organization for the effective management of personnel should organize jobs that fit people as well as assign people to prescribed jobs. Traditionally, organizational structuring identified work to be done, organized that work in the most efficient manner, and then hired people to do that work; bending and shaping people to the extent necessary to fit the jobs. But jobs are not that specific or definitive today. So much of work is knowledge work that we are acquiring people to do tasks and then must, to some extent, bend and fit the organization and resulting jobs to fit the knowledge of key people.

Organize Upward, Considering Flow of Work and Efficiency of Operations: The one facet of organizational work that has survived over the years is that work which is done at the operations level (in the factory and in the office) must consider equipment in place, the flow of work, and the most efficient procedures. The industrial engineer, the work flow experts, and the management engineers play the same essential role in this work now that they have for many years. This focus on the flow of work should pervade organizational thinking on jobs in the organization up to the level which approximates the then current college hiring rate for a person with a B.A. without prior experience.

Reconciliation: When the focus of the work is downward based upon management attention and upward by flow of work, and when it also requires an outward look toward customers and the effective management of people, there will come a point within the organization where these different focuses may come in conflict. At this point there must be a reconciliation. This is very pragmatic work and there are no guides other than common sense compromise.

Assign Responsibility for Organization Support Work: Organizational work is a general management job. But there must be support work for those doing that job. Those who do organizational work, for example, need information such as that which is outlined in this chapter. They may also benefit by the input and suggestions of those who have done a great deal of organizational thinking. For these reasons, organizational responsibilities for support know-how should be assigned somewhere. So much of what organizational structuring does involves the work and the effectiveness of people that it seems logical that this support work should be assigned to the personnel department.

Special Purpose Projects: One of the most useful basic suggestions with respect to organizational work is to undertake organizational work projects for a specific purpose. For example, you might set out to eliminate one whole level of management in your organization. A number of companies have, in fact, done

154

this successfully in the past few years. When this happens you eliminate a number of jobs, which reduces costs; you streamline the organization, which improves work process; and you increase greatly the quality of communications.

The Need for Quick Reaction: Organizational restructuring tends to be a very slow and bureaucratic process in most firms. Very often, the result is that the problem no longer exists or has changed in nature by the time it is dealt with. Be attentive, therefore, to the process of organization, assuring that there can be very quick reaction when needed.

The Delegative Method Applies in Organization Work: The delegative method, as described in chapter 2, applies, I believe, in organizational structuring work. There needs to be a policy management statement. There may be some requirements, though not many. The principal focus is on guides, information, and consultative services. Information technology provides the means for monitoring and control.

Delegate Considerable Responsibility for Organizational Work to the Manager of Personnel: The essential requirements for effective organization are knowledge of work and the skills and talents of people available to do that work. For this reason, the manager of personnel must make many organizational decisions. Normally, however, the manager of personnel will have to consult counterparts whose units interact with his own; needs guidance from the organizational support activity; and will likely have important organizational decisions reviewed.

Span of Management: The manager of personnel job should have basic responsibilities for essential matters of personnel, such as employment, pay increases, pay levels, training, et cetera for no less than 20 employees and generally no more than 100. This matter is so important that it might be an appropriate issue for a policy management statement.

Manage Transactional Organization: Recognize that many organizational decisions involve minor changes; but cumulatively, these organizational changes can impact the overall organization a great deal. For example, if a person leaves a unit, this may require an organization reaction; a change in organization recognizing the differences in experience and talent of the person who left and the new person who fills the job. That is transactional organizational work. Such organization decisions must be made by the manager of personnel who faces these day-to-day organizational issues. The firm must support such decisions because, cumulatively, they determine very much what the organization structure of the firm is.

Loose/Tight Controls: Organizational structuring must increasingly reflect the loose/tight style of management. In the absence of guidelines, control of organizational structuring has been extremely tight. All organizational structure changes in most companies have been reviewed and approved at very high levels. But with high-technology work, reviews by higher-level managers, who don't know the details of the work process, do not necessarily result in better organization.

The job to be done is to identify what elements or guidelines of organizational structuring need to be maintained on a controlled basis and which may then be delegated to managers of personnel. Work needs to be done in this area, but my own opinion, based on experiences in the past few years, is that the method of control should be to establish, at the corporate level, a *skeleton organization*. Within that skeleton, permit considerable latitude of organization decisions.

Matrix Organizations: Much has been said about matrix organizations. Sometimes the subject has been overemphasized, being set forth as *the* principle of organizational management. The fact of the matter is that every modern company has multiple organizations. These reflect, in part, the increasing specialization and the need to manage interdisciplinary knowledge. In personnel organizations, for example, corporate staff functional people are frequently assigned secondary responsibilities for overseeing all personnel matters in specified areas of the business.

Project Teams: Every firm also has project teams, and there are many of them in high-technology businesses. Project organizations cluster key people around specific projects. For example, an R&D unit may have a separate organization for each major product development effort. The key to project groups is to be certain that they have a special purpose and that they serve a real need. When that special purpose is accomplished, the project group should be dissolved. Only people with essential roles should be in the project organization. Membership in project groups should vary at different stages of the project.

Networking: Networking refers to the communications exchanges and informal working relationships which evolve in a firm. In doing their work, people establish these communication and work links simply to get things done in the most efficient manner possible. With management information systems there can be an enormous amount of networking in a company.

Because networking does involve communications and work relationships, however informal they may be, they represent an integral part of the organization of the firm. In its most positive form, networking involves people contacting and interacting with others in the firm who are the most informed or the best qualified to help get a job done. In its negative sense, networking can become uncontrolled and represent a form of organizational anarchy.

Networking is part of organizational structuring in companies today and will become more and more a part of the organization as the information and commuications revolution continues to evolve. Effective networking must be nurtured but, at the same time, controlled. There is still much to be learned about how to manage networking; but it is clearly an element of organizational structuring, and one guideline for proper organization is to consider networking.

Grouping: Companies are well-advised to apply the concept of grouping wherever possible. Grouping, in effect, involves decompartmentalization.

As more people have come to know more and more about less and less, organizations have tended to become more and more compartmentalized. Furthermore, these compartments tend to become increasingly isolated from each other, partially because of the unique technology and terminology of each field. Each group tends to pursue its own objectives for its own purpose, which frequently has little to do with enterprise goals.

Grouping means clustering specialist units with commonality of technology for effective operational direction and more effective management of people. The manager of grouped units likely adds little to the knowledge or work practices of any unit. Rather, it is an interdisciplinary management job, concerned with unit missions, resources allocation decisions, and coordination.

Organizational Picturing: The organizations that exist are recorded for information purposes. That recording also serves the purpose of a tool for analysis and improvement of organization.

The traditional method of organizational picturing has been hierarchical: the boxes and the lines. Such picturing still serves the purpose of information and analysis at the top of the organization and at the bottom. However, in middle-level jobs (from jobs equivalent in level to college-entry positions up to jobs reporting to heads of business divisions), hierarchical charting must be complemented if there is to be a true picture of organizational relationships.

One method of doing this is to picture the job itself, or an organizational unit, at the center. Then indicate individuals or units which report to that individual or unit, and those who the unit or individual report upward to. Also indicate regular external working relationships and regular working relationships with peers and others in the organization. With information techology, such picturing can be arrayed instantaneously.

Avoid Major Organizational Projects: In the past when a company turned its attention to organizational work, it very often launched a major project. The work could last for six months to a year and involve a lot of consultant work. Experience suggests that this approach to organizational structuring work is not effective. The tasks taken on are too vast. The results involve too much organizational change at a point in time. Organizational structuring work, like performance appraisal, communications, and other facets of the management of people, should be an ongoing activity.

Recognize That There Are Many Temporary Organizational Units: Because so much of organizational work should react to opportunities and needs (which themselves are temporary), it must be recognized that much of organizational structuring itself is temporary. Sometimes organization is designed only to accomplish a specific task or to meet a given situation. Where this is the case, it is extremely important to establish in some way a "sunset date" on that organization; a date when the organization would either have to be changed or disbanded.

Simulate Smallness: One of the advantages of a small firm is its quick reaction capability. Large companies can simulate smallness in some of their organizational work. You simulate smallness, for example, when you establish organization based upon businesses, divisions, profit centers, and units.

Neutralize Bigness: Neutralizing bigness is relevant when bigness cannot be avoided; when you cannot establish small profit centers and units. Essentially, what you must do to neutralize bigness is to neutralize bureaucracy; and this should be a guide to organization work.

Insulation: More and more work is being done in companies because it is required by outside organizations. For example, an enormous amount of work in the field of personnel is done to meet the government's requirements. Required reporting may serve some noble purpose; and it's essential to obey the law.

The problem is that there is a tendency to gather personnel information that shapes personnel practices based upon what is required by outside organizations. Yet what is required by them serves their purpose and does not necessarily contribute in any way to the effectiveness of work in your organization. This suggests the need to insulate work done for others from work done to improve the effectiveness of work in the firm. One way to do this is in the structuring of the organization.

Manpower Ratios: Utilize extensively both manpower ratios and organizational level guidelines. These are key auditing tools. Don't use them to determine what organization should be but rather to identify potential problem areas.

Organizational Fluidity: The organization of a firm must change at the same rate as, and be consistent with, the change in the business itself. Because businesses are changing constantly (a day at a time) there is a need for considerable fluidity of organization.

Organization work should rarely be a change agent. Change

occurs from such things as changing conditions, new products, and better management practices. These are the causes of business fluidity, and organizational structuring work must be geared to respond to such change.

Utilize Information and Communications Technology: The use of MIS in organizational picturing has already been noted. We are learning, however, that information and communications technology can be a tool of organization; because it accesses so much information relevant to organization. Without information technology it probably wouldn't be practical to keep track of the multiple organizations which actually exist in the company. Information technology facilitates monitoring of project groups. MIS provides information for analysis; and the possibility to develop and analyze different types of organization models.

Determine the Cost of Organizational Change: Every organizational change has a cost. It is a cost of disruption. New work and new working relationships are created, and it takes time for people to become effective in these new working relationships.

Transactional organizational changes responding to needs or opportunities represent a necessary cost to business. The cost is moderate; the need apparent; and probably it isn't worth the time to develop methods for estimating costs. What we need to do, however, is to determine the cost of major organizational overhauls. Simple guidelines will do the job. One project, for example, indicated that the dollar cost of major reorganizations equals one-tenth of the annual salary of all employees directly affected.

The Compelling Need Principle: We should change organization only when it is necessary. Too often, major organizational overhauls have simply reflected the interests of senior people; the bad advice of some consultant; or an executive putting his own stamp on the organization. Units are then moved around from one business to another; and different organizational relationships are established. But the result is simply "same monkeys, different trees." Be opportunity- and need-oriented.

Committees: Ideally, the only standing committee in a company should be the board of directors. This is a legal requirement.

160

We hold far too many meetings in business. But obviously there are times when people must get together to exchange information or because of some working relationship need. Then those who are directly involved should do just that. Necessary meetings are almost never perpetual, or even recurring.

In a very short time, ongoing standing committees will no longer serve the purpose for which they were originally created. They have become self-perpetuating, surviving long beyond their need. They tend to meet periodically, whether it's necessary or not. They are organizational mutants.

Conduct Practical Organizational Research: There is much still to be learned about organizational structuring and its impact upon effective work. Frequently in organizational work what appears to be the most logical organization is not, in fact, the most effective. The fact that there is much to be learned suggests the need to build methods of organization research into support work.

There are practical opportunities for organizational research. When a company has a large number of operations which are essentially the same, for example, try a different organizational structuring in one unit, and determine from operating results the effect of that different organization. We need to have other practical methods of looking at organization and analyzing it. There is a need to take these guidelines, or other guidelines, and examine them further to determine more specifically how they affect operating results. There also needs to be research on effective organizational structuring processes.

Avoid Redundancy: In every organization I have ever known, there are some jobs that are simply redundant. If you eliminated the job altogether it would make no difference in the operation of the business. In many large companies it's also not hard to find the same job being done in more than one place.

If you look hard enough in your own organization, you will find some redundant activities. Even if there are only a few of them, the elimination of redundancy improves operations. Constant attention to the problem of redundancy can protect against a cancerous growth of unnecessary work.

Organize Only for the Purpose of Organization: Never create an organization to get pay increases or to satisfy egos. Status is of value, but organization is a very costly way of satisfying the need for status. Don't neutralize an ineffective person by organizing around him. You are better off creating an organization of people who are effective and finding a place in that organization for each person to be effective.

Chapter 13

EMPLOYEE COMMUNICATIONS

For 35 years, surveys of personnel problems have always shown two subjects considered by most companies to be major issues requiring corrective action: more effective communications and workable performance appraisal. Over these years, just about every company has made major efforts at improving communications and performance appraisal. Each project resulted in better programs. But the better programs worked less well. When you perform an activity better and better, but find that it works less and less well, you must conclude that there is a problem of basic concept. Recent work suggests this to be true; the basic approach traditionally used by business in both employee communications and performance appraisal has been flawed.

BASIC FLAWS IN EMPLOYEE COMMUNICATIONS

The consulting work I have done in employee communications has focused on specific techniques and practices which will yield more effective employee communications. These, in turn, have been primarily responsive to specific company questions or problems. It has been a very pragmatic activity, resulting in a number of effective practices.

While the approach was extremely problem-oriented, there have evolved some basic ideas and principles of what constitutes effective employee communications. Probably most important, in my opinion, the work has identified a fundamental flaw of approach in employee communications in American business generally.

Like all communications, employee communications involve

163

the transmission of information and the receiving of information. The fundamental flaw in approach in employee communications has been the overfocus on the company as the transmitter of communications and all employees as the receivers of communications. It is my personal conclusion that employee communications should basically reverse these roles to be really effective.

Effective employee communications should involve the employee as the primary transmitter of information; for the most part, employees ask questions. The company's role is essentially that of a communications transponder.

The essential thrust of employee communications has been that, in a variety of ways, the company told employees things it thought they should know. When a company had "open communications," then it told employees a great number of things; if there were no open communications policy, then the company tended to tell employees as little as possible. But "open" or "closed" is not the issue; the issue is really the relevance of what is communicated.

Under traditional employee communications practices, the focus was on the company as the initiator and transmitter of communications. The company determined what information would be communicated, how much, and how. Then by written media, by telephone hot lines, in meetings, by audio tapes, by closed-circuit TV, and through supervisors, the company communicated massive amounts of information. The weak link in this communications avalanche was usually perceived to be the supervisor. Therefore, as companies tried to increase the effectiveness of communications, they generally focused on training supervisors in effective communications; mostly this meant teaching supervisors to say the same things, with essentially the same words.

If the transmission of communications then still seemed not good enough, there was a tendency for the company to communicate more and to make sure that what was communicated was more accurate. The emphasis then was to send information by more efficient methods; and to have more of the information communicated by top management and the central personnel staff. This, in turn, resulted in a higher proportion of communications in writing, with more of the writing being done centrally

164

so that it could better reflect the company's views and be less dependent on the supervisors for effective communications.

This traditional focus on employee communications is highly programmatic; and communications may have become the first casualty of the programmatic approach to managing personnel. The programmatic style was very efficient, but a programmatic approach to employee communications has not been effective.

Effective communications should ensure that employees know whatever is necessary in order to do their jobs well. Effective communications probably also means an attitude on the part of the company where employees have the right to know what they want to know about their jobs, their own careers, and factors which affect their jobs, their security, and their future.

With respect to work assignments and performance objectives, the "company" likely knows most about employees' needs for information; but here the "company" is the supervising manager and not the corporate office. But each employee also has specific and individual needs for information about his job.

Employees themselves understand best what they want to know. It is a gross error to think that all employees have an equal appetite for communications or that all have the same questions. Let the employee ask the questions (initiate communications). For a company to determine what employees *should* want to know is wasteful and somewhat arrogant.

This represents but a summary of the analysis and conclusions on basic issues relating to employee communications. The essential conclusion I have reached is that employee communications require a total revamping. The result should be a focus on rapid response in answering employee questions rather than essentially company-initiated communications. The implications of this simple conclusion are massive. Specifically, for example, the following would be general guidelines for effective communications.

1. Company-initiated communications should be far less than they now are, and essentially they should be restricted to: work-related information; basic company or business unit assignments and objectives; essential company policies; legally required information; and very little else.

2. The company should be organized and equipped to respond rapidly, accurately, and honestly to questions by employees.

3. Essentially, there must be a highly delegative posture toward employee communications. Companies must work hard to improve communications at the first levels. This means assuring that managers of people, who are the ones who receive most of the questions, have the resources to get information and the inclination to answer questions. The capabilities of line managers need not be to know the answers but always to have access to the answers. It is the managers who should be the primary receivers and responders.

4. When you consider efforts to improve communications, factor in current employee attitudes toward company communications.

5. There must be a system for unblocking communications obstacles and a safety valve to make sure upward communications are not blocked.

6. Monitor the effectiveness of employee communications.

COMPANY-INITIATED COMMUNICATIONS

There must still be some company-initiated communications under this different approach to employee communications, where employees generally initiate communications and the company is a transponder. If you follow this course, you will be surprised at how much less the company communicates. In cases I am aware of, the amount of company-initiated communications was reduced by as little as 20 percent to as much as 60 percent.

Company-initiated communications must be done very well. With a lesser quantity of communications, companies can and should concentrate on a higher quality of company-initiated communications. Here are some suggestions for improving the quality of company-initiated communications.

In the course of each year, each of your employees probably

receives written material that exceeds the number of words in all the regular issues and briefs of *The Sibson Report*. This is a great deal of written communications, and much of it goes unread. Employees probably receive an amount of verbal communications that are equal to what is written. Employees may have to listen to what is said but they don't have to hear it.

Even when a company reduces employee communications, there is still a great deal; and you may find there is still too much and have to reduce the amount of company-initiated communications even more. Your goal should be that the written word and the spoken word must be limited enough so that communications from the company are an event; and employees will tend to pay attention.

What the company communicates must be relevant. Communications that are initiated by the company must be on essential matters; for example, basic company policies and practices. Employees don't have to be expert in how the company does things; but they do have to know the basic objectives of the firm, and they do have to know basic policies affecting their work and their careers.

Information that passes through the employees' ears and eyes into the brain must be understandable. It doesn't have to be in cartoons to be understandable, but it must be in the language of the reader. Material written by lawyers and actuaries, or even material written for managerial or personnel people, can't always be understood by most employees.

Pictures (not cartoons) are a more effective communications medium than words; and the spoken word is more effective than the written word because there is an opportunity for dialogue. Most importantly, remember that there is a common method of communications; the English language. The dictionary is your reference, not the words you use with your colleagues. If you need advice on how to use the English language when communicating to employees, your best consultant is your local high school's 11th grade English teacher.

Communications must be believable. For any of it to be believable, all of it must be believable. The greatest sin of employee communications is one instance where the company, or one of its representatives, doesn't tell the truth. Even on small things, the company must be truthful to be believable. For example, if we're going to call salary increases "merit increases," then make sure they really are for improved performance.

Communicate to employees information that is essential in their work or important to them. You are communicating, not selling. Your focus should be on matters that are important to employees, not things that are important to management. Managers, out of pride, sometimes overemphasize communicating good things about the company.

A company must be attentive to the vehicles of communications. Every firm needs to have (or have access to) a communications specialist: one who knows which method of communications is most effective for a specific purpose. Employee communications experts should be in the personnel department. Never have public relations people involved in employee communications. Also avoid "staged" communications productions. Employees instinctively distrust "media events" by their company, and often wonder about the purpose of these productions.

Remember that what a company does is part of communications. If you preach quality at the work station but sell products which are designed to be of poor quality, you have contradictory communications. If the company says it values long service but reduces employment by induced early retirement, you have contradictory communications. In all such cases, employees will likely believe what happens rather than what is said.

Every firm could use some "great communicators." We have seen vividly in the political area the value of a person in a leadership position who is a great communicator. A company could use that skill, not just at the corporate level but in each business area and at each location. Ideally, this would be the top manager in each instance. But not all excellent managers are excellent communicators. Alternately, there should be some other person who carries out the role of the great communicator. Look first in the personnel organization.

Make sure that basic channels of company communications are effective. Organization, for example, is a critical element of communications transmission; which is one reason why organizational structuring is a vital element of effective work. The effectiveness of communications is somewhat in inverse proportion to the number of organizational levels.

Be alert to developments in communications technology. A great deal has been written and said about the information revolution and its impact on the management of personnel. There is a companion revolution in communications; and it too will massively affect management. Fiber-optic technology will mean thousands of closed-circuit television channels. And if you can "dial a prayer," employees could also "dial an answer." If the networks can poll the American public by telephone, you can do the same: within 24 hours you could have every employee express an opinion on a matter of great importance, at a very low cost.

THE COMPANY TRANSPONDER

A transponder is a communications mechanism which transmits a reply promptly upon receipt of a message. That's basically what I want the company to do; respond promptly (and accurately) to employee questions.

Here is an ideal case. One large firm has many locations all over the country. When an employee has a benefit claim, he goes to a first-level personnel generalist; or, if necessary, the personnel generalist goes to the employee. The benefit forms are completed, and the benefit coverage explained. Within 24 hours the personnel person transmits electronically the claim information to the corporate office. It is processed, mostly by computer, a check is electronically drawn on a local bank, and delivered to the employee by the personnel person. The average time for handling claims is three days, and every claim is discussed and explained.

I think every firm should have a formal system for handing employees' questions and complaints, when the employees think it is necessary. But such a system must result in *answers*; and I think that it should never take more than two weeks from the day the question is entered into the system until it is answered, regardless of how many steps are involved.

Identify the transponders in your firm. Make sure they are working and that they provide answers promptly. Recognize that, in most companies, transponders are the managers of personnel.

MANAGERS AS COMMUNICATORS

Good communications may well be a company objective, but it is not necessarily an objective shared by all the managers who must do much of the communicating all the time. Sometimes, *managers may want to communicate poorly.*

Communications take time, and good communications take a lot of time. If a manager doesn't communicate or spend much time at it, the time saved can be spent on something else. Good communications aren't always visible, and the manager may not get much credit for good communications. If you don't communicate something, then you know something others don't know, and that may be of value to you.

If you're not really sure of a subject and don't have the time (or don't want to take time) to learn enough about it, you may be well-advised not to communicate it. It may seem better to the manager not to communicate at all than to do it wrong.

There aren't many risks to the manager for not communicating well. How many times in your firm has a person been terminated or given 1 percent less in salary for poor communications? Also, there are excuses for poor communication. For example, "She doesn't remember" or "He didn't understand what I said" are very good and generally accepted defenses for not communicating or for communicating poorly.

In much of our communications work, there is the assumption that all managers want to communicate well and that they will do so only if they understand how to do it and we help them. The fact of the matter is that in some ways good communications with employees may be contrary to the self-interests of some managers much of the time and all managers some of the time.

First levels of supervision *have* been a principal problem of effective employee communications. Too many who are now supervisors of personnel are not qualified to do the communications job, which is one reason for establishing the job of "manager of personnel." Qualified managers need support, which is one reason for having a first-rate personnel generalist available to every manager of personnel. You must also make sure that each manager knows that he must do this job, and that his performance will be evaluated, in part, on how well it is done.

170

CHANGING EMPLOYEE ATTITUDES

Don't assume that employee attitudes toward company communications to employees are favorable. Supervisors may want to communicate poorly; employees may not want to listen.

Employee receptiveness to communications, whether company-initiated or as responses, is very different from company to company. The level of receptiveness is a function of many variables; but the most important by far is past employee experience. It is worth some effort to get a realistic sense of the attitudes of employees toward communications from your company before an effort is made to improve communications.

Here is one company case, and it is not the worst case I have ever seen. This company had off-site meetings with groups of employees conducted by consultants. Here are the reported results.

- Most employees think the company doesn't really care much about what they think or what they want to say.

- All employees are disinclined to communicate openly with their supervisors, even in those cases where they like, respect, and admire that supervisor. They think that open, upward communication would probably not be effective and that it could cause them trouble.

- All think that opinion polls conducted by the company are a charade and that they fail to pose many important questions.

- Employees think that most downward communication is highly selective, largely propaganda, and generally boring.

- Many examples were given where the company says one thing and does another.

This is a very brief and unscientific sample of employees' views on communications in one case. Until you know what your employees' attitudes are, you might reasonably assume that your employees have somewhat the same view.

MONITORING COMMUNICATIONS

Like other facets of personnel, there needs to be monitoring or auditing to be assured that effective communications are occurring. Monitoring of effective communications need not be complex. One company reported a method of monitoring the effectiveness of employee communications. It is such a simple method that it deserves consideration.

The communications monitoring involved two parts. One part was a questioning approach. Twenty supervisors would be selected, and each of them would be asked the same ten questions. These were questions that employees would likely ask their supervisor, and each supervisor was to answer the question as he would answer it to an employee. Each of these sessions took about 20 minutes.

There were also sessions with 20 employees. In this case, ten statements were made, and the employees were asked whether they agreed, partly agreed, or disagreed. They were also invited to make comments. Each of these sessions also took about 20 minutes.

The second part of this monitoring of employee communications involved a one-hour presentation on the part of location management and personnel people to corporate personnel about how they were now conducting employee communications at this location. The location management was asked to send in advance all relevant documents or illustrative material relating to their employee communications activities. Then there was a meeting, and location management made a presentation. After this formal presentation, the location management and personnel people would be asked to provide specific cases where lack of effective communications or improper communications caused a problem.

This is just one case. Some firms think that opinion polls or focus surveys will, among other things, provide satisfactory monitoring of employee communications. My experience has been that communications monitoring must be highly customized to each firm.

I urge firms to work on sampling, as one tool in communications monitoring. Why not use the same demographic sampling techniques used by political pollsters as a basis for more in-depth polling of employee thinking, attitudes, understanding, and opinions? With sampling methods, interviewing as well as written responses could be used to gain an understanding of the effectiveness of employee communications.

There must be safety valves and a system for unblocking communications. It need not be as dramatic as was the case at IBM, where every employee could directly contact Mr. Watson. But there must be some method of assuring that needed communications do not get blocked, garbled, or short-circuited.

Normally, the question and complaint system will assure that roadblocks to effective communications are removed. Don't take that chance; have some safety valve system. Here's one suggestion: tell employees they may write directly to the personnel vice president, on a confidential basis, whenever they think it's necessary.

In your monitoring system, keep before you the goals of communication. The goals of employee communications are two-fold. First, communications should be good enough to contribute to effective work. Second, communications must reasonably satisfy employees' desire to know. Measuring success against these standards is difficult. A company will never have perfect communications. The goal is to be good enough.

Chapter 14

PERFORMANCE APPRAISAL

Just about all managers and personnel professionals would agree that performance appraisal is essential to the effective management of personnel. Almost all firms have had formal appraisals of some type at some time; and most have them now. Performance appraisal is much discussed and studied by personnel professionals. Every year the improvement of performance appraisal programs is among the high-priority items of many personnel departments. Yet an appraisal of performance appraisal would usually still result in a rating from completely inadequate to moderately successful.

BASIC ISSUES

Performance appraisal is a vital personnel activity with *two basic objectives:*

- First, performance appraisal is essential to rate the performance of people as one basis for various personnel actions; including merit pay increases, identification of candidates for promotion, transferring of personnel, assessment of various personnel data, and manpower planning.

- Second, performance appraisal is essential to evaluate performance in order to determine actions which should be initiated to improve performance and thereby increase the effectiveness of work.

For clarity, "performance appraisal" will be used as a broad generic term, covering any type of appraisal for any purpose. "Performance rating" will refer to the sole act of concluding how good performance is, without explanation or analysis. "Evaluative appraisal" will refer to the analysis of performance, essentially to determine how performance can be improved.

The basic conclusion about performance appraisal, which came out of work on the "developmental project" on management development and succession, is that the essential reason why performance appraisal is less than satisfactory is that the two basic *objectives* are incompatible if dealt with in a single program or process.* Therefore, the rating of performance and the evaluation of performance must be separate processes.

The basic premise is critical; it was basic to the evolution of the new approach to performance appraisal. "Proof" of the proposition is more experience and understanding than scientific. In my opinion, the reasons for this premise are overwhelmingly correct.**

There is another basic issue with respect to performance appraisal. In practice, "performance" has too often been unclear. Frequently, for example, it means how well a person does the job he is now assigned, his potential for the future, and his personal attributes. Performance of currently assigned duties and potential for the future are two very different things. Personal attributes don't necessarily have anything to do with either.

A person can be superb in his present job and have no future potential at all. Similarly, an individual may have great potential for future growth but is not performing very well in his present job. There are almost an infinite variety of combinations of performance and potential; which is one reason why it is so difficult to deal effectively with performance and potential in one appraisal program or process.

There are also some important procedural reasons why performance and potential cannot be rated or evaluated at the same

---

*Actually, many performance appraisal programs have additional objectives which complicate the problem and are incompatible themselves with at least one of the stated objectives of performance appraisal.
**See *The Sibson Report*, Spring 1983; pp. 2-4.

time or by the same process. For example, the immediate supervisor, if qualified to manage personnel, is best qualified (and perhaps the only one qualified) to rate or evaluate performance. But the immediate supervisor is rarely qualified to rate or evaluate potential, which may involve consideration of positions higher than the supervising manager has experienced or where potential is in a field that is foreign to the supervisor.

For clarity, therefore, "performance" will refer to how well the job now assigned is being done. "Potential" refers to the ability to acquire additional know-how and skills to become qualified for future higher-level jobs.

Thus, in what has been treated as a single activity—performance appraisal—there are actually four distinct and noninterchangeable activities which cannot be done at the same time or by the same process. Effective "performance appraisal" then involves: performance rating; potential rating; evaluative appraisal of performance; and evaluative appraisal of potential.

PERFORMANCE RATINGS

Performance rating has a single objective: to determine how well each person is doing the work now assigned. The rating is a conclusion, best expressed numerically. There is no need for an explanation of the conclusion when the rating is made. Only the conclusion is vital.

Performance ratings should be viewed as an essential piece of personnel *information*. Performance ratings result in information which is vital to the management of personnel. Most companies, for example, have the desire to pay top performers more than others. Performance ratings can be critical as a guide to achieving this objective and as a monitoring system.

Performance ratings are also essential data for the personnel department. Such ratings are a critical input to a firm's human resources information system. Such data can also be important in the monitoring role of a corporate personnel department. For example, the data may indicate an area where management is failing to take performance into consideration, in the proper way, when making personnel decisions.

The extraordinary thing about performance ratings, which only call for a conclusion without analysis, commentary, or written description, is that they are remarkably accurate, provided that there are no more than five gradients of rating. Performance ratings that only call for a numeric conclusion are also remarkably simple to do. A manager can rate the performance of 20 people in 20 minutes. Another 20 hours of discussion won't change the ratings much. If the same manager rates the same people 20 weeks later, the ratings are essentially the same, and again it only takes 20 minutes.

There are a number of ways in which performance ratings can be obtained. One method is to give a manager a list of all employees whose work is known to him. The list is separated first by immediate subordinates; then other subordinates; then others whose work the manager has had a chance to observe; and finally, those who have been observed casually or intermittently. Next to each person's name, the manager makes the rating, on a one-to-five gradient scale.

These ratings are done most effectively if someone from personnel is present. The role of the personnel representative is to focus attention constantly on what is being rated: how well the person does the job now assigned. The personnel representative can also be helpful by asking the "why" questions and by making cross-comparisons. Even in this type of a session, 20 people can be rated in 20 minutes.

Sometimes, of course, little things can be very big. In the case of performance ratings, the labels put on the one-to-five scale can be extremely important. One set of descriptions that has been used in a number of firms defines performance-rating gradients as follows:

1) The level of performance that would be expected of a qualified person who is new in the position; acceptable level of performance.

2) Intermediate.

3) Work is done to the standards of performance set for the position.

4) Intermediate.

5) It is difficult to see how the position could be performed better.

Methods are available to audit or monitor the simple system that has been described to ensure that the resulting numeric ratings of performance are valid. Each individual's name will appear on the performance-rating lists of a number of supervising managers. Thus there are multiple ratings, and this is a monitoring tool. Performance rating results for units can be reviewed. If the results do not show an expected distribution or a reasonable distribution of ratings, then those performance ratings should be examined. Performance ratings for each unit should be compared with productivity measures and measures of business results of the unit. If, for example, performance ratings are high and productivity and business results are low, then either the performance ratings are incorrect or the quality of management of such a unit may be deficient.

The relationship between performance conclusions and personnel actions is a sensitive issue and one that has caused problems in appraisal. Personnel professionals know that there will be inconsistencies between performance ratings and personnel decisions, because in any personnel action a number of factors must be considered. In auditing performance ratings, personnel professionals follow-up only when there are frequent inconsistencies or when a pattern needs to be examined.

Performance ratings are easy to do, but they are extremely difficult to explain or discuss with those who are rated. In this system, however, there is no need to discuss the ratings with any employee. Rating conclusions should generally *not* be disclosed to employees. Discussions of performance ratings may serve no purpose, are always extremely difficult, and are sometimes counterproductive. In this recommended approach a manager may conduct performance rating feedback sessions, but it is not required.

Of course, employees (especially supervising employees) would know that ratings were being made. They *might* ask what their ratings were, and such questions cannot be ignored. In such cases (which are rare in actual experience), the supervisor can explain the rating in terms of the definitions. For example, a supervisor might point out ways in which the job was not being performed to standard.

The requirement is that managers make performance ratings. Managers are also required to *consider* their own ratings when they make various personnel decisions. Performance on the job is, for example, a critical consideration in granting salary increases; though not the only consideration. The manager's own conclusion about performance should be used by that manager in a number of key personnel decisions.

POTENTIAL RATINGS

There is also a single objective for potential ratings: they should show the potential of each person to assume higher-level responsibilities sometime in the future. Again, there is no explanation or analysis required; potential ratings only record conclusions. These can also be expressed numerically.

Potential ratings are also essentially an information system input. These ratings are useful for making various types of personnel decisions. They are also important in analyzing personnel data; for example, in monitoring the relationship between potential ratings and subsequent promotions.

Procedurally, potential ratings and performance ratings can be obtained at the same time and essentially be a part of the same process. Potential ratings by the managers of personnel reflect their opinions. These need to be reviewed and final judgments made at a higher level.

Potential ratings lack the precision, validity, and reliability of performance ratings for a number of reasons. Performance is observed but potential is an unpredictable future speculation. Furthermore, potential is dependent upon the individual's aspirations and willingness to make the time investment usually necessary to "get ahead." However, these ratings are used in matters covering a period of time. Therefore, potential ratings can be monitored from time to time to see if each individual is, in fact, demonstrating a degree of potential consistent with the potential ratings.

As with performance ratings, the labels attached to the five gradients of potential ratings are important. These also must be business-related and positive. One set of definitions used successfully is as follows:

1) Career-peaked.

2) Intermediate.

3) Potential for one or two promotions in same area of work.

4) Intermediate.

5) Potential so great that it cannot be determined, either in terms of the amount of potential or the direction of career growth.

At times, potential ratings need to be supplemented by more sophisticated methods of determining the potential of employees. This is particularly true of those in the early stages of their careers and where there is consideration of a change in a career path. In such cases, the individual might be subjected to an in-depth interview by an experienced personnel professional. This is also an appropriate time to consider psychological assessment.

The methods of early identification may also be applicable as a supplement to potential ratings. These would apply to younger and less experienced people.

There need be no feedback of potential ratings to employees. Like performance ratings, communications to employees on this subject can be difficult and frequently negative. But this is company information for company actions. There isn't any need for ceremonial feedback. If people know that potential ratings are being made, they may ask about their own ratings. If pressed, the supervisor will have to tell them what their potential ratings are, as positively as possible.

EVALUATIVE APPRAISAL OF PERFORMANCE

Evaluative appraisal of performance involves any activity that examines why performance is at its current level. It may examine strengths and weaknesses; accomplishments and failures. All this is done in relation to observed and/or demonstrated work as performed in currently assigned duties.

Just as performance ratings have a single objective (recording conclusions as to how well the job was done), evaluative appraisal of performance also has a single goal; to determine personnel actions which would improve performance.

Actually, some type of evaluative appraisal is going on in an organization all the time. A person does work and the supervisor evaluates it, and when he thinks it appropriate or has the time, the supervisor says something or does something to improve performance.

Periodic evaluative appraisal is a conscious company activity. It is a formal review; a time to rethink and consider observations which have been made. It is a required activity; at predetermined intervals to ensure that it occurs. Evaluative appraisal reviews what has been observed and learned since the last evaluative appraisal. It calls for determination of formal and planned personnel actions to improve performance wherever that is possible and appropriate.

The process need not be applied to each person. For example, those who are doing their jobs as well as they reasonably could be done need not be evaluated. Those about to retire or those who are about to be assigned to another job should not be subjected to evaluative appraisal.

Performance rating conclusions serve not only the immediate supervisor but also the corporate office and, therefore, they must be submitted to the corporate office. Evaluative appraisal, on the other hand, serves only the immediate supervisor. Records of evaluative appraisal should not be sent to anyone. Higher-level managers and the corporate office need only know that evaluative appraisal is being done and what resulting personnel actions are planned to improve performance.

Evaluative performance appraisal is a very complex process, and the results are inevitably imperfect. The job is made simpler in this approach, however, because of the singleness of purpose of the activity. The only objective is to identify a personnel action, or a few such actions, which would likely result in improved performance. Unlike traditional performance appraisal, therefore, this approach requires no elaborate, complicated, or comprehensive process. The purpose is not to learn a lot about performance, create some inventory, or even understand behavior. The objective is only to identify actions which would likely result in improved performance.

The presence of a personnel professional can be extremely helpful during the evaluative appraisal process. There aren't many occasions when operating managers need the information, advice, and support of qualified personnel people more than when they are called upon to analyze the performance of subordinates and make decisions as to what should be done to improve performance. The personnel person who participates in such sessions gains experience from each session which should be useful in other sessions; and he learns of successful actions which have been taken in similar situations.

It is the manager of personnel, however, who must do the evaluative appraisal of performance, decide on the personnel actions, and who is then responsible for seeing to it that they are implemented. The supervisor may have to rely on others, such as the training department, to implement some of the actions decided upon. But both the actions and their implementation are clearly the essence of the management of personnel.

The evaluative appraisal process is a very simple and direct one. Performance ratings indicate those whose performance can be improved or whose performance has declined and whose work should be evaluated to see what personnel actions should be taken to deal with lower levels of work effectiveness. The evaluative appraisal process determines personnel actions designed to improve performance.

It is extremely important to consider personnel actions and not training activities alone. The purpose is not to build a training agenda but to improve performance; and the personnel actions best designed to accomplish that objective are what is needed.

One or a very few personnel actions to improve performance should be identified for a person and not a whole laundry list. It is difficult enough to identify and implement one or a few such actions to improve performance. The correct personnel action in some cases may be simply to talk to the employee. The most effective personnel action may involve restructuring the job. In other cases, the personnel action might involve changes in organizational structure or work procedures, transfer to another job, or some change in the physical environment of the job. Some personnel actions will involve training.

In practice, less than half the personnel actions planned as a result of evaluative appraisal of performance involve training of any type. Typically, only one of four training activities planned involves any kind of group training.

Frequently, the decision which results from evaluative appraisal of performance is to do nothing. This may be because the supervisor cannot think of an appropriate action. It may be because, in the judgment of the manager of personnel, improvement of work must come from within the employee. Perhaps, in the judgment of the supervisor, a person may not be capable of higher levels of performance.

Formal feedback communications sessions are not an essential part of evaluative appraisal. When personnel actions are planned, however, this may require communication with the employee in some manner. These communications sessions are easy for the manager and the employee. They are always positive, because they involve discussions of actions which may help the employee work more effectively.

There is the last essential step. The personnel actions planned must be implemented during the year. They may be implemented by the supervisor, the employee, members of the personnel department, or some combination of people.

For various reasons, not all action plans are accomplished. There may not be the time; unforeseen events may interfere with implementation; or the action planned may not work. But many get implemented, and performance improves.

EVALUATIVE APPRAISAL OF POTENTIAL

Essentially the same process is followed for evaluative appraisal of potential as was described for evaluative appraisal of performance. The two can be done as a single process; but for performance, higher-level managers merely review personnel actions, whereas, in fact, high-level managers, supported by senior personnel staff members, must make potential rating decisions

183

and assume accountability for evaluative appraisal of potential.

Development of potential involves knowledge about plans for the development of the business in the long run, a broad view of the business, and a broad knowledge of companywide opportunities for individuals. Furthermore, actions initiated as a result of evaluative appraisal of potential frequently require a commitment of resources and people not available to most managers of personnel.

Evaluative appraisal of potential ultimately involves determining personnel actions to develop people's capabilities in a way to meet the future needs of the business. This requires an evaluation of the business as well as evaluative appraisal of people with potential. Evaluation of potential has no relevance without an answer to the question, "Potential for what?" Potential is evaluated to learn who can be developed, and in what manner, to meet the future needs of the business; and to create a pool of talent to select successors to those now holding higher-level positions.

Part of evaluative appraisal of potential must also necessarily consider the individual's ambitions as well as potential. Fulfillment of one's potential requires commitment; generally a substantial personal investment of time and effort; and sometimes involves personal consideration, such as relocation. Not everyone is willing to make such investments.

As in the case of evaluative appraisal of performance, the evaluation of potential has as its "product" the identification of personnel actions. In this case, however, the actions are a series of activities and plans to give the person opportunities to acquire what is thought to be necessary new knowledge, additional skills, and required experience which he would not get in his present job. Personnel actions to develop potential involve a long-range plan to meet the future manpower needs of the business.

Evaluative appraisal of potential and determination of personnel actions need not be done for many. The developmental route for many people is set; their career paths are in their job families or areas. The plant foreman moves up the factory management ladder; the engineer moves to senior engineer; and so it is in many areas. These cases represent a high percentage of developmental activities in a firm, which is why career pathing is such an important matter.

Evaluative appraisal of potential and the determination of personnel actions for development and succession can be limited to those few who are potentially the next generation of executive management; for the "fast-track person" and for the unusual specialist, either in a recognized academic discipline or one of the increasing number of business disciplines. This generally represents less than 3 percent of total employment.

The process described is one way to meet the future manpower needs of the firm; and evaluative appraisal of potential, with resulting personnel action plans, is the cornerstone of that process. This is a simple, low cost "succession" program. It is a system that works.

THE APPRAISAL SYSTEM

What has been described and proposed is a system. It is a complex system for personnel professionals. For managers in the operations, it is a number of simple activities which seem relevant and which are a natural part of the job of the manager of personnel.

The performance appraisal system overall is illustrated in Exhibit 14-1. This system is a series of ratings and evaluations, rather than a frantic once-each-year action of filling out forms, following procedures, and engaging in difficult, unpleasant, and frequently counterproductive discussions with subordinates.

Performance appraisal becomes four distinct activities, each with a single purpose, rather than one multipurpose dinosaur. There are performance ratings and potential ratings; which are essential information systems. There is evaluative appraisal of performance to determine personnel actions to improve performance on current jobs. There is career pathing for those who have potential, and there is evaluative appraisal of potential for the limited number who must be given special knowledge and experience that would not come from normal growth in their fields of work.

This process makes the critical separation of rating and evaluation, and the combination of these mutually incompatible activities has been one of the basic reasons which has caused performance appraisal to fail. The process also makes the important separation between actions to improve performance of currently

assigned duties and activities to develop people for future identifiable responsibilities.

Exhibit 14-1

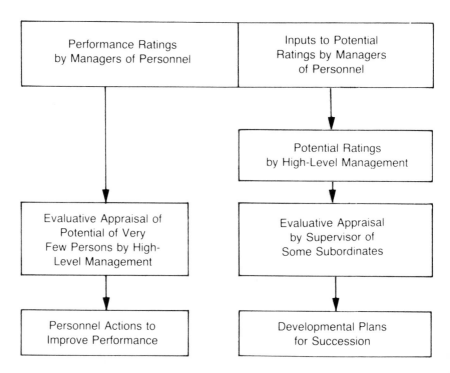

The result is a performance appraisal system rather than a
program. Requirements of managers are few, understandable, and
attainable (e.g., they must make performance ratings on a five-gradient system). Under this approach, performance appraisal is a
means to a number of clearly identifiable and attainable objectives; providing needed personnel information, improving performance, and meeting the future manpower needs of the firm.

Chapter 15

TRAINING AND DEVELOPMENT

Employment has to do with the acquisition of the key assets of the firm: human talent. Training and development have to do with human asset enhancement. In this context, training and development are a vital part of the effective management of personnel.

TRAINING-DEVELOPMENT

Sometimes the management of personnel could be improved by details. One such detail, which if nothing else would assist in communications on personnel subjects, would be to make the language of management more precise. In fact, I have long urged the development of a business dictionary which all firms could then reference. An example of this need for more clarity in the language of management is in the confusion and the interchangeability of the words training and development.

When I use the word training, I mean instruction and practice to make an employee more proficient in his currently assigned duties. Therefore, training has to do with increasing the effectiveness of people's work in their current jobs. Development has to do with the creation of new capabilities or new knowledge to qualify an individual for some future higher-level position. No doubt, training and development are interrelated. Becoming more proficient with current assignments might (or might not) make one better prepared to assume some future position at a higher level. Learning new knowledge and skills to perform some future higher-level position might (or might not) also contribute to greater effectiveness in a currently assigned job. For me, the focus of training is on today's job: the focus of development is on some future job.

When you examine company training activities, you may find that many items have little to do with making people more proficient in their current jobs. Training of this sort is wasteful. It involves a costly expenditure of company funds for no demonstrable business purpose. Training not specifically geared to better work performs no service for the person either and, in fact, might create false expectations.

It's more difficult to evaluate the real value of many developmental activities and whether they are serving a business purpose, because development necessarily involves long-term goals. If you look at development activities practiced in many firms you will see people learning new skills and getting better at some facet of management without any clear goal in mind in terms of enhancing qualifications to fill some future position which is likely to exist in the firm.

By the nature of their work, many who specialize in the field of training and development are very articulate and persuasive. They can identify some relationship between any training activity and capability and proficiency. They can make any proposed developmental activity sound essential to the future of the business. Apply the three criteria that are necessary for any personnel activity: clear need; action-result; and cost-value. When this is done, many training and development programs that exist would not get a passing grade.

In much of what is written and said about training and development, there is also too narrow a view of this activity. Too often, training and development means what the training department does. In fact, however, training and development activities developed, monitored, or conducted by the training department represent a very small portion of all the training and development that goes on within any firm. Most effective training is not programmatic.

NONPROGRAMMATIC TRAINING

A substantial amount of employee communications is a most elemental form of training. There are communications with employees about their jobs, what their jobs are, how to do their jobs, and what is expected. There is work-related information; people are told why their job is done and how their work affects the work of others.

Communications about work standards and objectives represent an important part of job communications, which is also basic training.

The reaction by a supervisor to work done and suggestions for improving work may be labeled performance appraisal, but it is communications that represent the essence of training.

Anyone who reads these words is a supervisor or is supervised, or is both. From your own experiences, think about what job-oriented communications or the lack of them have meant in terms of training and the effectiveness of your work. Isn't it true that those who are told well almost always do better work than those who are not told, told poorly, or told incorrectly? Clear and useful communications about what to do, how to do it, and how to do it better are the cornerstone of effective training.

Operational training and development is a phrase coined to describe that one-day-at-a-time training which occurs in the normal course of the work operations. These activities are not very often thought of with respect to training, but they are the essence of the activity. More effective work communications and nurturing the operational training and development which occurs in every firm are, in my opinion, the greatest opportunities for improved training in any company, and this effort would have little, if any, incremental cost.

Continuous teaching, coaching, and counseling go on in work operations. Supervisors are constantly showing employees how to do their work or explaining to them what they do not understand. Supervisors advise people in work problems or talk to them about their working relationships. All of this involves operational training and development.

Ideally, every task should represent a learning experience. Each learning experience usually adds only incrementally to the know-how and skills of a person. These experiences are, however, happening constantly; in the course of a year there are 100 or perhaps even 1,000 such events.

By the very nature of operational training and development, it is the director of work, the immediate supervisor, who is the trainer. A major effort on the part of the manager of personnel should be to have each supervising director develop skills in operational training. Such skills of making daily work experiences into training experiences may be a basic characteristic of leadership down in the organization.

In my opinion, personnel departments should continuously focus their primary attention on this facet of training and development. I don't think it's likely to be accomplished by a new training program; although some skills training in operational training and development techniques would help. Operational training and development really happen when personnel generalists in the organization, looking at each director of work as an individual, help that person develop this critical skill.

People are learning all the time. On their own initiative, many people learn things which represent substantial amounts of training which actually occurs in an organization. Such self-training is very deliberate and conscious on the part of some people. They observe what others do, they reflect on an experience, they think about how to do a given task better. People who do these things are making every work experience a learning experience.

A lot of learning occurs off the job. Employees may do some reading on an entirely different subject and learn something that helps them in their work. They may also learn from material, either written or spoken, in another field which creates a new understanding about their work. Much learning about managing people and personal relationships occurs from exposure to things outside the personnel field. Speaking from my own experience, I learn something about interpersonal relationships every Sunday morning.

Some employees have very formal and conscious agendas for self-learning. I know of no study that has ever been made on the subject, but I suspect that there would be a very strong correlation between the amount and intensity of self-learning and the success of people in their fields.

Self-learning and employee-initiated training and development are thus an important part of the overall training which occurs in any firm. Frequently, however, it is done on a rather random basis. Employees may be directing their efforts to learn things which are of little value to them; they may be learning the wrong things; or they may have the wrong priorities. There is, therefore, a need to give direction to and nurture self-training.

Companies have, of course, financially supported self-learning activities through tuition-refund plans and by purchasing magazines and periodicals. Perhaps most of all, however, individuals need counseling on how to focus their self-learning activities. I don't think this can be done from a central training department. I think that such direction and advice must come from the manager of personnel, who would be assisted in this work by the personnel generalist. On occasion, the manager of personnel may ask the personnel generalist to deal with this matter directly.

Personnel actions resulting from evaluative appraisal for improving performance represent another substantial portion of the total training effort in the company. Personnel actions from evaluative appraisal reflect specific needs and opportunties for learning or the acquisition of knowledge or skills. They have been planned because they should result in increased effectiveness of work. This is highly cost-effective training.

If you added together training that occurs because of work-related communications, what has been described as operational training and development, self-training, and personnel actions from evaluative appraisal to improve performance, I expect that you would have 90 percent of all the training which occurs in a firm. None of it is planned or directed by the corporate office. At best, the corporate training people are facilitators and provide advice and consultative services from time to time.

Nonprogrammatic training is the essence of training in any business. It isn't the kind of activity that's very dramatic. It isn't the sort of thing where people in the personnel department can list items in their reports to get high grades with their management. Nonprogrammatic training doesn't cause much excitement at a meeting of The American Society of Training Directors. But nonprogrammatic training represents the essence of activities directed toward increasing the effectiveness of work in any business.

Work-related communications, nurturing self-development, operational training and development, and personnel actions to improve performance resulting from evaluative appraisal all represent the essence of management. Companies that seek to improve the effectiveness of their training should look first at these areas. This is where most of the training should occur and, in fact, is occurring, for better or worse. Improved activities in nonprogrammatic areas cost very little. Improvements also become part of that management process and tend to be self-developing. My advice, therefore, is to get your training experts to focus their attention primarily on improving nonprogrammatic training activities.

Last year, I worked with a firm on its training activities. As part of this work, the company's personnel people determined what training was going on and how training dollars were spent. Their conclusions were: 95 percent of the training which occurred was nonprogrammatic, but 95 percent of the money spent on training was on programmatic training. In this case, it was because their training people only knew how to do programmatic training.

PROGRAMMATIC TRAINING

There will always be a need for some programmatic training. For example, some of the personnel actions which result from evaluative appraisal indicate training needed by a number of persons. In such cases, it is cost efficient to have all those with the same training need learn in a common training session, either conducted by the company or by some outside party.

There is also a great deal of what I call "trades training." For example, it is necessary to train tool and die makers by formal courses of instruction. There is some element of "trades training" in just about every job family. Sometimes this training is required in very high-level positions.

Training programs are also necessary when some element of the business is changed, and many people affected by this change must learn new things. When a new computer system is installed, for example, people must be trained how to use it.

Group training resulting from identified personnel actions, trades training, and special training caused by changes in the business are all clear needs for programmatic training. In even the largest company, however, you won't find many such programs necessary. Yet in many of these firms, there are dozens of training programs and thousands of training sessions.

As a practical matter, many of the training programs which are conducted are implemented because some training professional, either inside or outside the firm, believes that it is in the interests of the company (in the interests of every company) to undertake such training, and top management is sold on the idea. Some of these activities have involved massive undertakings. There has been a long parade of such training panaceas; from decision-making courses to sensitivity training. Companies expended large amounts of money and enormous amounts of time on such programs. On balance, in the opinion of many personnel professionals, these programs didn't do much harm; but they cost a great deal of money.

From this experience, companies should be far more cautious in the future than they have in the past about programmatic training activities, unless there is a very clear need. Yet in many firms I know, there is still a fascination with programmatic training. When you visit these firms and talk to them about training and development, they bring out lists of the training programs they hold.

Simply making people smarter or more sensitive or better in their interpersonal relationships does not necessarily improve the effectiveness of work. For the individual, for example, who is already overly sensitive in his relationships with others, further sensitivity training may detract from his effectiveness of work. Why make everyone take reading improvement training, when some are already very good readers and others have bad eyes? All canned programs, including all programmatic training, represent answers. Rarely, however, do large numbers of employees have the same training needs. The needs of each of us, at any point in our careers, are highly individualistic.

There are those who argue that there are some special skills which should be taught in all companies. Basic supervisory skills training, enhanced communications skills, and basic teachings in the practice of management are examples of special skills urged on all companies. There is surface logic to this view; but such thinking is a basic flaw in company training. Every supervisor needs supervisory skills, but some are already very skilled. Some who need more supervisory skills need training in some other area of their work much more. Some supervisors are barely good enough, but they wouldn't get better if you gave them supervisory skills training every month. Finally, how can you develop a skills training program that deals with everyone's deficiencies?

A few such programs, early in a person's work career, are helpful. Even in these areas, remember that while skills training has value, such sessions also involve a cost; principally a time cost. And in skills training programs, the most critical thing is to assure that the items are all relevant; not a list of the things the trainer knows.

Those who work in a firm also need a basic understanding of the business. The need to know the business will vary with different jobs, but everyone should have a basic knowledge of the essentials of the business they work for. This is illustrative of an important item of programmatic training which requires little time; for most employees, one hour of instruction in this subject every five years would likely be sufficient.

Finally, there are certain outside courses which are helpful. These include professional meetings, seminars, and special courses at universities. Companies have learned to manage these training and development activities quite well, primarily because there are out-of-pocket costs associated with such programs. Also, people must be away from work, so it is a very visible training activity with a very clear time cost.

DEVELOPMENT PROCESSES

You can't separate training from development, but the focus in this chapter so far has been on training. Training improves current performance and has to do with productivity. It is the clearest and most demonstrable need for activities. Greater productivity is a very high-priority item in most firms.

Developmental activities are less urgent, if for no other reason than they deal with the expected future needs of the firm. Clearly, correct identification of such future needs is very important. This is at the heart of the problem of effective development activities in many firms. Development should aim at meeting predictable needs. Such predictions are very difficult, even if the correct process is followed, and they are always somewhat incorrect. A second major problem of developmental activities is that there is far less certainty of success than is true in training activities.

In consulting assignments, I have wondered many times whether the basic thinking about development is not also flawed. I think that this is particularly true of management development.

There is a tendency to start with a laundry list of knowledge, skills, and experience thought to be required by every successful manager. Candidates for management development are selected rather early in their careers and are then the beneficiaries of such development. If successful in prescribed development activities, a candidate is then deemed qualified to be a manager.

My principal reason for thinking that this (admittedly broad-brushed) picturing of traditional management development is flawed is that it hasn't worked very well. Most really successful managers never went through the process. Many who have gone through the process aren't successful. Studies have also shown flaws in each basic part of the process; but that is something which needs to be explored further, and it is another item on my personal "developmental project list" for the future. For now, I can only urge companies to be cautious about this traditional approach to management development. I think there will be fundamentally new approaches to management development emerging shortly, just as there have recently been new approaches in communications and performance appraisal.

There is only one legitimate business purpose for any developmental activity. This is to fill future jobs. This must involve filling reasonably predictable open jobs in the future.* It involves

---

*Never attempt to predict every future job. Instead, identify job categories (i.e., top financial positions).

succession: people within the firm succeeding to higher-level positions. The ultimate objective of development is successful promotion from within.

Succession is essentially selection. When a job opens, the company looks inside at the candidates available and picks the best qualified person. If no one is qualified, then the company has to go outside to recruit: succession has failed.

Essentially, a firm should do developmental work only to assure that there are qualified candidates to fill jobs that become open in the future. I think this is a basic concept and the key to more effective development activities in the future.

If people learned everything required to move on to the next higher-level job, then there wouldn't be a need for any developmental activities at all. But we know that doesn't happen; and it doesn't happen, to a greater extent, as we get to higher-level positions in the organization. It is for this reason that there must be developmental activities; to give people knowledge and skills that are not required in their current assignments and not learned in their current work, but which will be required if they are to become viable candidates for future higher-level job openings.

Effective succession starts with career pathing. For most levels of the organization, career pathing is development and succession. Career pathing occurs at all levels of the organization. It occurs even at the lowest levels. For example, high school graduates hired as clerks become senior clerks, bookkeepers, administrative assistants, etc.

Career pathing means moving people from one job to another in a logical job path or career path. Career pathing may involve special training or assignments, or even job redesign, so that a person is better able to fill the next logical position. Essentially, people become qualified for the next career path job when they perform well in their current job.

In all cases, people are moving in their career path as openings occur. People are being consciously directed in a logical manner in their careers so that the work experiences they have, complemented by some special training or instruction from time to time, assures a sufficient number of qualified candidates for higher-level jobs when they become open.

Personnel professionals must always be attentive to just

exactly what the logical career paths and job families should be. At any point in time in a hierarchy of jobs, there are also multiple directions in which the next logical career move might be made, and this must be analyzed. Managers of personnel and the personnel generalists who support them must know these alternate career path directions.

One of the most difficult parts of career pathing is to identify the proper time for distinct changes in career paths. For example, you don't wait for an engineer to become the highest-level non-supervisory engineer before you start moving him into engineering management; it may be too late, and it may be too costly. Therefore, it is important to determine at what point in each career path people should be considered for different career path directions.

These types of decisions can be determined by personnel professionals. But actual selections, be they a transfer or a promotion, which represent career movement and career pathing must be made deep in the organization by those who know the jobs and who are responsible for the work. These are the managers of personnel, supported by the personnel generalists.

In lower-level positions, vertical movement from one job to another in a logical career path involves selection from among each person who has had prior experience that is relevant to the job being filled. Typically, for example, a person will have done 90 percent of the tasks to be performed in the new job, even though it was done at a more junior level. The prior work is directly relevant to the work which is to be done, and the prior work experience is a valid basis for making selection judgments and predicting the success of an individual in his next logical career move.

As you get higher into the organization, more and more of the total job to be done will involve tasks which are different from anything that has been done before. A person will never have performed some of the duties in his new job. Therefore, prior experience becomes less important as the sole basis for making selection decisions. It is at this point that special developmental activities must be considered, not only to prepare people for higher-level positions, but to assess their abilities and the likelihood of their success.

PROFESSIONAL DEVELOPMENT

There are a number of unique features in professional development. None of them, however, is more essential than continuing education. Professional people's work is knowledge work. They are educated at college levels before they start working. Because of that professional education, they can do professional work the day they start to work.

In their career paths, professional people get a continuing education, partly from experience in applying the knowledge they learned from their formal education and also from special courses, professional journals, and from other professionals. In many professional fields, a point is reached when professionals must either make a career change or they need more education or reeducation. Their career change may be into the management of professional persons in their discipline or into other areas of business where the professional's knowledge would be of value, such as engineering marketing.

For those who stay in knowledge work in many professional positions, there is a point when technological obsolescence occurs. In the physical science disciplines, for example, it has been noted that most of the basic research breakthroughs have been made by engineering people during the first ten years following graduation from college. What happens is that beyond that point, in rapidly changing technological areas, the technology changes so much that the academic training of the individual has become obsolete.

Clearly, the answer is reeducation. In some disciplines today, it is not sufficient to have this reeducation through a few special courses at established universities or company sessions. Increasingly, there is a need to actually have people "recertified": reeducated so that they learn the technological advances that have occurred in their field since the date of their graduation. In many of the high-tech fields, I think we will find that established educational institutions will conduct on-site educational courses to meet this technological gap. It represents a substantial business opportunity for the academic world.

MORE THOUGHTS ON MANAGEMENT DEVELOPMENT

Never underestimate the degree of failure reflected by going outside the company to hire key managers. The cash recruiting cost is enormous; at least a full year's salary. But there is a second cost; the impact on the morale and the attitudes of people within the organization. Furthermore, some studies have shown that the track record of people recruited from outside the firm, even those with great reputations, has been very poor. In many ways, when a large corporation goes outside to fill a key spot, there is a form of business bankruptcy; there has been a major management failure.

This is one reason why firms have put so much effort and money into management development programs. A few large firms have even established their own in-house universities, primarily to develop their future management and executive groups.

Many of these company programs in management development involve a substantial cost. They require a great deal of time on the part of those subjected to the sessions. If, in fact, the result of those management development activities is that jobs are filled successfully by candidates within the company, then the value would be justified even if the costs were very high. However, every such program I have know has contributed little, if anything, to successful succession.

We now know one thing that does work, and therefore I would recommend, first and foremost, that companies utilize the process of evaluative appraisal of potential and the development of personnel actions to develop people to become qualified candidates for reasonably predictable open jobs in the future. It is the process related to performance appraisal which has already been described.

This is a very low-cost system of management development and of providing for effective management succession. It is a highly effective method. It is, however, probably insufficient. Used alone, this process would not reasonably assure management succession. There is a missing link; another item for future exploration.

EXECUTIVE TRAINING

We don't hear much about executive training. It is too often assumed that the same principles and practices which apply to other employees apply to executives also. My experience is that there are some very unique and special techniques for effective executive training.

The whole notion of developing executives is not really relevant. Most executives are career-peaked! For what job would you be developing your CEO? Executives need training, not development.

In fact, executive training is closely related to the problems and strategies of the business. Determination of executive training needs may start, therefore, by examining the strategic and operational needs of the business. In the process of determining these needs, it is important not to confuse ongoing information needs with executive training needs. There is a continuing need for executives to have better information and a better quality of information in order to make necessary decisions. Executive training needs relate to gaining new knowledge or skills to perform their existing executive jobs better.

Executives, themselves, must be the primary source for identifying executive training needs. If they don't think they have any training needs, no training will occur. You can't even lead these horses to water.

There are some special executive training practices which have proven effective. One method of increasing the effectiveness of executives in dealing with specific strategic needs is through organizational structuring changes. Much of the organization of the company at the top is designed to utilize existing skills of key executives. Changing the organization at the top to optimize executive skills, in the light of special business situations or to achieve special goals, is natural and simple.

Another effective executive training technique is learning by the experiences of others. Company problems are seldom without precedent. This being the case, one method of executive development identifies other businesses that have had similar situations. This could be done by business research. Those companies are then studied. It is rare that the resulting information is directly applicable to your firm. Rather, the experiences of others represent a background of information that will help your company's executives deal with their own situation more effectively.

Executives frequently receive some form of coaching or counseling. Hopefully, members of the board of directors are selected so that they have something to add to the knowledge and experience of top executives. Some companies have hired consultants to give special needed knowledge.

Executive development can also occur through exchanging information with other key executives. Too often, executive interchange of information is on a random basis: those persons an executive knows; because they are friends, on a common board, or play golf together. I think much could be accomplished by channeling and being selective about executive interchange of information. Identify other executives whose knowledge and experience would be valuable to your own executive group; and vice versa. Consciously develop information working relationships which will support executive training.

Chapter 16

PRODUCTIVITY IMPROVEMENT

The objective of the management of personnel is effective work: high levels of employee productivity. Productivity is then an ongoing effort of management, rather than some special effort. Nevertheless, faced with declining productivity and increasing uncompetitiveness, in the 1970s many firms launched major efforts at productivity improvement through more effective human resources management. Such experiences have heightened know-how about productivity, which, in turn, adds to our knowledge and experience in the effective management of personnel.

MANAGEMENT OVERVIEW

Our business system has performed a miracle in increasing productivity. It is the increase in employee productivity over the years that has led to the very high standards of living in our country.

Traditionally, companies have increased productivity in one of two ways. They have substituted capital for labor, or they have methodized work. Increasingly, however, these are marginal opportunities for increasing productivity in many businesses. Until there are technological breakthroughs, the major opportunity for increasing productivity in the near future for many firms will be through more effective human resources management.

Productivity improvement efforts are no different from any others. They should be evaluated as part of the normal business process of requests for investment and capital resource allocation decisions. At any given point in time, unfortunately, productivity improvement activities can be rationally viewed as postponable. The difficult question is, How long can productivity work be postponed? Eventually, postponement may seriously detract from the achievement of company goals.

Allocation of resources to productivity improvement involves very little, if any, commitment of capital. Cash expense commitments are very moderate. The major commitment of resources is with respect to *time*; mostly the time of operations workers and managers in your firm.

It is possible to tell management what resources have to be committed to achieve a targeted increase in productivity improvement through more effective human resources management. The problem is that the *results* of these activities must necessarily be *estimates*. No one can guarantee that, for a given commitment of resources, some concrete result will occur in terms of any measure of business improvement.

There are, however, general methods of assessing the cost effectiveness of productivity improvement work through human resources management. For all their imperfections, quantifiable elements of input and expectations of output can be presented to evaluate projects to improve productivity through personnel management actions. These are imprecise, but the result usually shows such enormous potential gain for moderate investments that such projects represent a prudent business risk.

BASIC ACTIVITIES REQUIRED TO
INCREASE PRODUCTIVITY

Companies have successfully increased productivity through better management of personnel by using many different programs and practices. Their experience suggests, however, that there are some things which should be done before specific programs or practices are undertaken. These activities should be "in place" if any productivity improvement activity, based largely on the more effective use of human resources, is to be successful. Here are the "basics."

You Must Be Able to Measure Productivity: Before any specific program is undertaken, it is essential that some measure of productivity be established. These should be established for the company overall, for each major business unit, and preferably for each unit or profit center. Unless you have measures of productivity, how will you know whether any action you undertake to increase employee productivity has worked? Furthermore, managers have found that the development of productivity measures helps to focus on the determination of what productivity is in each unit, department, and business function.

You Must Be Willing to Commit Resources: Increasing productivity through more effective human resources management doesn't cost much. However, nothing is free, and appropriate resources must be committed. Generally, there are no capital expenditures in productivity improvement work through personnel management. Cash expenses, including consulting fees, should be moderate. The major cost is time; time committed to productivity work that would have been used to do something else.

Make Employee Productivity a Part of Every Manager's Job: Increasing productivity through more effective management of personnel is a manager's job. Therefore, the job must be assigned to every manager. Those managers must be told that it is part of their jobs. Furthermore, they must be given time to do the job. Most managers will also require some support; such as information and advice from members of the personnel department. Finally, in order to make the productivity improvement job a part of every manager's responsibilities, it is necessary to measure, at least in part, their performance, based on how well they manage productivity.

The Company Must Pay the Human Costs of Productivity Improvement: There is a human cost which results from any successful activity to increase productivity. For example, if productivity is increased there may be a need for fewer people; and this may mean that someone must be laid off. The reward for improving operations can't mean loss of employment. Success in productivity improvement also requires change, and this change can cause problems for some employees. For instance, employees may be transferred from work they have done effectively to work they find more difficult to perform. There are various human costs of productivity improvement. These costs must be anticipated; they must be managed; and they must be paid for by the company.

There Must Be an Organization for Productivity Improvement: Like any other ongoing activity, there must be proper organization if productivity improvement is to be accomplished. Each manager is accountable for the productiveness of employees in his unit. There must also be a support organization. Support work for productivity improvement through human resources management is logically the job of the personnel organization. Companies err if they establish another hierarchy to do this work. However, in the initial phases of such work, some companies have found it helpful to establish, *on a temporary basis,* an individual or group at the corporate level which is accountable for monitoring productivity improvement work, to act as "facilitators," and to give early momentum to the work.

Productivity Improvement Requires a Long-Term Plan: Successful improvement of productivity through better management of personnel takes more than a year. Therefore, there must be a commitment to do the work over a period of time; usually three to five years. This is not to say that productivity improvement work requires the same effort each year. But there must be some continuity to the work until the results which have been planned are accomplished. Companies cannot start up and shut down productivity improvement work. If they do shut it down, it will be extremely difficult to get it started again.

MEASURING PRODUCTIVITY

It is probably correct to say that productivity cannot be improved unless it can be managed. It is doubtful, however, whether productivity can be managed unless firms know what it is. And if they know what it is, it must be measurable. Productivity can, in fact, always be measured. Some measures may be crude, but they are useful and usable.

There are four basic approaches to measuring productivity:

• Physical volume

• Dollarized productivity

- Value added

- Proxy measures of productivity

Physical Volume: The productivity measures developed in a machinery division of a large corporation would serve as one example of productivity measured by using physical volume. Work standards had been set at each work station, and the actual physical volume of parts produced or assembled was counted daily. Thus, for each worker, each section and each department, there was a daily count of physical volume and hours worked.

In another firm, the company produced three basic products; which, in combination, represented 90 percent of the total physical output. The firm developed a "key productivity index"; a weighted index of the physical output of these three products divided by man-hours for each product.

The industrial engineering department in another firm determined through its studies that the production time for product A was equivalent to ten units; for product B, six units; and for product C, three units. With these weightings and the numbers of units of work produced, they had a measure of total physical volume of each.

Another firm had 84 retail stores that performed various repair and maintenance functions. Employees kept records of the time spent on each product serviced and the type of service rendered. This was a basis for measuring employee productivity in each of the retail organizations.

Dollarized Productivity: Dollarized productivity volume is by far the most universally usable and most comparable measure of productivity. Current accounting practices can keep records of the total sales for the business and each operating unit. Total dollars of payroll or total man-hours of work are also kept by the same units. These records provide dollarized productivity measures for the company overall and for each of its principal subdivisions.

Value Added: The value-added measure of productivity is by far the most difficult and complex. In effect, it measures the total dollar value of goods shipped or produced or services rendered. It subtracts from this number, however, the total dollar cost of all materials purchased. The difference represents the dollar value added to the product or service by the people who work in the operations.

This number can then be divided by the number of people, man-hours of work, or dollars of payroll to get productivity measures. While a complex approach, it is felt by some to be the most valid basis for making comparisons of productivity trends between different type of businesses.

Proxy Measures: There are various types of proxy measures of productivity. These do not measure productivity directly, but they do provide measures which are likely to be reflective of productivity trends or correlate with trends in productivity.

One proxy measure is a composite of performance ratings. Companies that have rated employees' performance in their present positions with a numerical conclusion can calculate the average and median performance for the company overall and for each of its operating units. If these ratings are conducted periodically, then a trend of performance can be established; and this change in levels of performance is a proxy measure of productivity increase or decrease.

Another productivity proxy measure is employee cost. The pay of people is a measure of their value; therefore, cost can be indicative of value. A weighted average of people by job level for each volume of sales or level of output is a rough proxy measure of productivity.

Some operations of a business provide a service. In these cases, the service can be assumed constant, and therefore the denominator alone becomes a measure of productivity.

Usable Measures of Productivity Can Be Established: There are many ways to measure employee productivity. Anyone could look at each and find contaminants and imperfections. But there are imperfections in any data in a business, including such common personnel data as turnover and pay trends. There are, of course, also many imperfections in standard accounting practices. Such imperfections, however, do not mean that the data is not useful. Even imprecise data can serve a useful purpose. Imperfect data, used properly, is usually more useful than no data, provided the cost of getting and reporting the data is in line with its value.

A few years ago, there was a very dramatic case of what can

be accomplished in terms of measuring productivity. The management of a large chemical company had a commitment to increase employee productivity, for business reasons somewhat unique to its own operations. One of the first steps taken by top management was to mandate that every division, every location, every section, and every unit of the company would have to develop productivity measures, even units such as corporate law and plant cost accounting.

Rather than embark on a monumental project with costly specialists doing the work, management was advised to have the units evolve their own productivity measures. This was thought not only to be most cost-efficient but probably most productive, because in analyzing units, it is the knowledge of the operation itself which so often proves to be the key to developing usable productivity measures.

As a result, there were training sessions and information briefings throughout the company. The company developed a few cases to illustrate the kinds of work that could be done in developing productivity measures. Following these sessions, each unit was charged with the responsibility of developing a productivity measure.

As would be expected, there was some complaining and some feeling that "it couldn't be done." Top management persisted, and it was done. Productivity measures (237 in all) were developed in every unit in that company within six months.

METHODS OF INCREASING EMPLOYEE PRODUCTIVITY

There are now over 40 specific practices or programs which have been used to increase employee productivity through more effective management of personnel. Many of these are variations of the same basic method. Therefore, it is most helpful to think of the basic methods of increasing employee productivity; and ten of these are summarized in this section.

Management Style: A company would not likely develop and implement a managerial style for the primary purpose of increasing employee productivity. The managerial style that exists, however, can materially affect employee productivity.

A highly proceduralized style of managing people will impede effectiveness of the management of personnel and will probably cause diminishing employee productivity in most firms today. This is a "key issue" for most firms; and the reason why many are evolving from a highly proceduralized system of managing people to some form of a "delegative" management system.

Management style can also affect productivity when that style includes setting high expectations. Generally, companies with high but achievable goals and expectations are likely to have more high-achievers and higher achievement. The company that expects greater productivity will probably get improved productivity.

Management style can also be used as a method of increasing productivity by establishing examples for lower levels of supervision. If higher-level managers will take actions to increase *their* productivity, then lower-level managers are likely to do the same.

There are some cases where the company's corporate management style requires each operating business to develop specific actions for increasing productivity as a part of the business planning process. Productivity improvement plans must be specific in terms of what is to be accomplished, the methods which are to be used, and milestones of accomplishment which can be used by the corporate office to review progress toward achievement of these goals.

Product Design: The product or service may be redesigned to make the business less people-intensive and thereby increase employee productivity. A classic case was the redesign of large grocery stores to be self-service stores. More recently, gasoline stations have done the same thing. There have also been dramatic recent cases in large entertainment resorts and major appliance manufacturers, where the business has been redesigned to be less people-intensive, with resulting increases in employee productivity.

Employee-Initiated Work Methods: The most widely publicized basic methods of increasing employee productivity through human resources management involve employee-initiated work methods. These include such specific programs and practices as participative management, quality circles, semi-autonomous work groups, and open systems of management.

Each of these particular practices has its own characteristics, its features, its advantages, and its pitfalls. All of these, however, are based on one premise: the person who does the job knows something about the job that others do not, and, therefore, that person has unique knowledge and ability to initiate more effective work methods. This premise is clearly true for management and knowledge-worker jobs. It is also true of an increasing number of jobs in offices and factories.

Unproductive Practices: One of the most direct approaches to increasing employee productivity is simply to remove or reduce unproductive practices. There are many practices that evolve in any firm which detract from productivity. If they are removed or diminished, productivity increases.

Many of these unproductive practices were the proper thing to do at one time. Businesses change, but the practices and procedures of the firm do not always change accordingly. There is a great need for simplification of procedures in business today.

Some activities are inherently unproductive, even when they are necessary. Meetings of all kinds fall into this category. Every company has many meetings. Some are essential, some are questionable, some are recreational, and some are unnecessary—representing an escape from work. Even meetings that are necessary generally lend themselves to increased productivity by more effective management of the meetings.

Management Engineering Methods: A number of techniques have evolved, which are quite similar to the industrial engineering methods applied successfully in factories, that may be used to increase productivity anywhere in the firm. There are also some management engineering methods which were especially evolved to increase productivity through more effective management of personnel. One such method is time analysis. This technique, which can be applied very simply, at least identifies how people spend their time, so that time utilization can be compared to work priorities. Job redesign is another management engineering method of increasing productivity. Work is redesigned to utilize people's skills better and for greater efficiency in work.

Best-Practices Methods: Companies have increased productivity by learning from the experiences of others. Sometimes this is the experience of others in their own firm; sometimes it is the experience of other firms.

A company with many field locations, for example, can identify those particular locations where productivity is the highest. A study of practices in that location may indicate methods of managing people that can be applied in other locations, resulting in increased employee productivity.

The same technique can be utilized to benefit from the experiences of other firms. Such exchanges occur frequently at personnel meetings and conferences. Intercompany information can be more productive for some purposes if the exchange of experience is between firms with similar economic and operating characteristics.

Managing Quality: Managing quality involves practices designed to get each worker and each group of workers to do the right thing the first time. If nothing else, doing work correctly the first time eliminates subsequent need for rework. These practices have just recently been explored by some firms. They are based upon the fact that quality of work is part of the productivity equation in the contemporary firm. If quality can improve, productivity will improve.

Leveraging Knowledge: Companies have been managing knowledge and knowledge workers for a long time. As the number of knowledge jobs and knowledge workers increases, the effectiveness of the management of knowledge workers is becoming a more important aspect of improving productivity.

Companies have learned to "leverage knowledge." This means using a very small portion of the highest level professionals' knowledge and experience in the overall solution of a problem or in the accomplishment of a job. This is a productivity improvement practice.

Companies are also evolving information systems to increase the effectiveness of knowledge work. These are information systems which not only record printed information but also the experiences of professionals. These are fed into an information system, and every professional then has access to the knowledge and experiences of every other professional.

Productivity Bargaining: Unproductive practices in union contracts have been well-publicized, and this is clearly an opportunity to increase employee productivity among unionized workers. Less publicized, but sometimes just as important, are the time costs involved in contract administration. A number of companies have worked effectively to increase the productivity of unionized workers through productivity bargaining in a well-thought-through and organized manner.

Group Work: Increasingly, personnel problems are not unique in each company. Productivity improvement is one example. Many companies are now working to increase productivity through the more effective use of human resources. Such work involves some basic information and studies of value to many firms. Therefore, a company that is starting now to improve productivity through personnel management methods should keep in mind that the "study" has already been made. If it has access to information already accumulated by other companies, it can get right on with the job.

To the extent that companies can work together, within the constraints of existing antitrust laws, to deal with personnel problems which affect all of them, they will increase productivity. Firms can at least exchange information and experiences. They may work together on some problems; or hire a third party to do the work for all of them.

THE MANAGER'S JOB

Almost ten years ago, I made my first presentation on improving productivity through more effective management of personnel to a group of managers of a large international food company. After my presentation, there was a question and answer session; and the first question was a speech—a long and very emotional speech.

The thrust of the operating manager's speech was that managing people was a manager's job; and getting high levels of productivity was clearly a part of that job. My response was to thank him, and I have been thankful to him many times since. That speech always reminded me of who I was and what my job as a personnel person was.

Of course, it is the manager's job to hire people, make pay decisions, communicate and train; and do everything else relating to people at work. I trust that nothing written in this chapter detracts from that reality.

I pointed out to that manager that my presentation, like my job, was to help him do his job. My presentation, and all the consulting work I subsequently did in productivity, was to bring more knowledge to the managers of personnel, or provide them with tools and ideas to do the productivity job more effectively.

Personnel work is not just support and advice. There are no "staff" jobs in business anymore. Personnel persons have areas of accountability—operational accountability. Sometimes the accountability is direct (e.g., negotiating a contract) and sometimes indirect (e.g., recruiting employment candidates). Personnel people also set personnel requirements; those which relate to the law and those which relate to corporate business needs. Personnel audits managers; for example, there cannot be productivity at any price or by any method. The operating and auditing work of personnel does not change its essential role: to support the managers of personnel in every facet of "people at work." The effectiveness of the personnel department must primarily be measured by the effectiveness of managers of personnel. In productivity improvement, the essential job of personnel is to provide knowledge and tools, which managers can use, that contribute to higher productivity.

THE PRODUCERS

One way to increase employee productivity greatly is simply to increase the number of producers in your company. No one, to my knowledge, has ever done this; or ever considered doing it. Increasing the effectiveness of work by increasing the number of producers is, therefore, just an idea at this point in time.

You can categorize work, and workers, in any number of ways. Consider this categorization:

• Producing work: Activities which directly impact designing, producing, marketing, or distributing a product or service.

• Support work: Activities essential for the producers to do their work (e.g., plant maintenance).

- *Managing:* The point has been made that just about everyone does some managing today. Count here only jobs where the key activity is management of producing work or support work.

- *Other work:* Work not covered clearly by "producing work," "support work," or "managing."

I have had an opportunity to look at a few company cases, and I have been able to compare the distribution of work 35 years ago with what it is today. The data is shocking; and I suspect that these few cases are typical of American businesses in general.

What has happened, a day at a time, is that, to paraphrase an old British song, the world of work has been turned upside down. Thirty-five years ago more than 90 percent of all work (as measured by payroll) was producing work or support work; about 5 percent was managing work; and about 5 percent was other work. Today, not much more than half of all work is producing work or support work; about 15 percent is managing work; and almost one-third of all work is "other" work.

One cause for the enormous increase in "other work" is the government. We will assume here that everything the government has done is wise and serves a noble purpose. However, there must also be an awareness of the *cost* of governmental requirements. Today, the equivalent of about one of ten people in a firm does work directly or indirectly for the government.

We must evaluate this form of cost of government along with all other taxes, as individual worker-voters. But companies could take initiatives in reducing the proportion of "other work" the company created. I think that it could be the greatest single productivity improvement program ever undertaken.

Some part of the growth in "other work" is also due to increasing technology; but not very much. Far more is due to executive-initiated company practices. Executive management has, one day at a time, looked inward and companies have increasingly been preoccupied with administering themselves. There is also an increasing fascination with accounting, tax, legal, and strictly administrative matters, rather than customers, products, and quality.

214

You can see this increasing allocation of resources to "other" work even in personnel work. We spend far less of our time on subjects like effectiveness of work and excellence in the manage ment of personnel; and far more on such areas as the newest gimmick and tax loop-holes.

SOME LESSONS LEARNED
IN PRODUCTIVITY IMPROVEMENT

In the past few years, employee productivity in many firms has been increased through more effective personnel management. As would be expected, company success has been mixed. Some firms have experienced outstanding success. Others have made substantial progress. A few have had only moderate success. None has reported failure.

The experiences gained by these firms represent a body of know-how and useful experiences for future work. Here are some of the reported lessons learned through experience in productivity improvement through more effective personnel techniques and practices.

1. There is now in existence more than enough knowledge in the field of personnel to make improved productivity through more effective human resources management practical. Companies have had difficulties and have frequently struggled in their efforts to increase employee productivity through more effective personnel practices. No case has been reported where there were difficulties because of the lack of necessary personnel expertise.

2. In some respects, work to increase productivity through personnel efforts has simply been a matter of "looking down the other end of the telescope." Traditionally in personnel work, when firms have been confronted with some personnel problem, they have modified their personnel practices in order to resolve that problem. Sometimes, the fall-out value has been increased employee effectiveness at work. The reversal of this process is a practical way of improving produc-

tivity. The first question can be how to improve employee productivity. Practices are then designed to accomplish that objective. Frequently, the fall-out value is more effective personnel programs.

3. Sometimes very simple things are extremely effective. Many companies started their productivity improvement work on the assumption that anything that might be accomplished would necessarily involve very complex and sophisticated activities. Quite the opposite has been the case. Some of the great success cases in productivity improvement have involved very simple practices.

4. Productivity work should be done in manageable projects. Some companies have erred by taking on very open-ended productivity improvement efforts. They have spent large amounts of time and money thinking about what to do and organizing themselves to do it, but accomplished little.

5. Before undertaking some activity to increase employee productivity, evolve a system for measuring results of the project. Improving productivity means exploitation of opportunities. Sometimes these objectives are vague rather than geared to a specific and obvious problem. There is the question of whether the expenditure of time and money committed to the productivity improvement activities really paid off. It may be difficult to demonstrate the value of productivity improvement work unless some system for measuring the effectiveness of the work is established in the first place.

   One useful idea is to adopt an investment approach to productivity improvement. Manageable projects are undertaken, and systems for measuring or judging results are established. As each project is completed, the value to the firm is estimated, and part of the gain is reinvested in the next productivity improvement project.

6. The organization for improving productivity can be as important as the specific practices which are used. Productivity

work is almost always a project-oriented activity, with the nature and membership of each project group varying as different phases of the activity are accomplished.

7. There is little need at this time for more research in the area of productivity improvement through human resources management. There is still much to be learned, but the learning process is most likely to occur by utilizing and applying knowledge which now exists. Experience gained in applying known practices will represent additional learning experiences. Involvement in productivity work may result in new technology. The real opportunities for learning will now come from involvement in experiences rather than additional research.

8. Most productivity work that is successful is done in the operations rather than in a home office group. The closer those who do productivity improvement work are to actual operations, the more likely there will be success in productivity improvement. There may well be one or a number of members of the project team from the corporate headquarters or from outside consulting firms. But the work must be done at the plant, sales office, or engineering laboratory level. Furthermore, the project group must include people from that location who know its operations.

These are a few of the lessons which have been learned in productivity improvement work done in a number of firms. Perhaps one of the most important lessons learned is that these activities really do work. Another important lesson learned about productivity improvement work is to do it. For a firm deciding that productivity improvement is important and that the principal opportunity for improving productivity is through more effective personnel management, as contrasted to improved methods or capital substitution, that firm should start to work. The time is for doing, not for talking.

Chapter 17

PERSONNEL PLANNING

Personnel planning is an important and practical part of the effective management of people. Personnel planning has also become an integral part of the operation of personnel departments in an increasing percentage of *Fortune*-listed companies. Personnel planning is a practical activity because companies are doing it, and some of the results of this work have been helpful in making key decisions or evolving strategies for improving the business.

WHAT IS PERSONNEL PLANNING?

There are different types of "personnel planning." There is operational personnel planning, which is done each fiscal year in most firms. There is strategic personnel planning, which most often covers a five-year period. In each of these activities, there are input activities and application activities.

Operational personnel planning involves next year's events or changes. Some of these items are used in developing the operational plans or budgets of the firm. An example would be the determination of appropriate salary increase budgets for the next year. This is operational planning input work. Once the operational plan for the business and each operating unit is developed, personnel must examine the elements of that plan to see what items require personnel actions. Assignments must then be made to deal with these items. This is operational planning application.

Strategic personnel planning involves the identification and analysis of events or changes which will impact the business over a long period of time. Many of these need to be identified so that they can be considered as an input to the evolution of the strategic business plan. Some personnel planning items, however, may not have relevance to the strategic business plan, but they need to be identified anyway, so that the personnel department can anticipate and take appropriate actions at the proper time to deal with future changes which will impact the firm's ability to manage personnel effectively.

The focus in this chapter is strategic planning input. Other facets of personnel planning need be so customized to each firm that little can be presented which will be of value to any firm. Strategic planning application work, for example, is strictly a function of each company's strategic plan items.

THE IMPORTANCE OF STRATEGIC
PERSONNEL PLANNING

It seems elementary that personnel planning is as important as planning with respect to any other subject of management, if people are indeed important assets of the firm. Most managers would agree with that statement, but they will not support formal personnel planning until convinced that there are methods available, at a reasonable cost, for doing personnel planning effectively.

We know how to do personnel planning today. It can't be done with perfection, but it can be done about as well as firms do planning for many facets of the business. The skills and know-how for doing personnel planning are good enough, and companies that do this work will tend to do it better each year.

Conditions affecting the management of personnel have been changing rapidly in the past 35 years, and the rapid rate of change in conditions will probably continue or even accelerate. Companies have been hurt in the past, because without effective personnel planning, they could not deal in a timely manner with important changes that affected the management of personnel. In fact, one of the reasons strategic personnel planning is now being practiced in some companies is because those firms were hurt by their failure to do personnel planning in the past. Many senior executives, for example, feel very strongly that they should never again be surprised by such things as ERISA or EEO, *both of which were predicted in a personnel planning document written in 1966.*

Strategic personnel planning is also important because it deals with *opportunities* as well as *problems.* For instance, an understanding of the change in the mix of the work force and the resulting increase in knowledge workers was why some firms improved their methods of managing knowledge workers and developed more effective recruiting practices for such positions. For some firms, strategic personnel planning information was the basis for evolving successful business strategies or for developing new business areas.

SOME GUIDELINES FOR EFFECTIVE STRATEGIC PERSONNEL PLANNING

Strategic personnel planning is a relatively new area of business activity. It is an area where some companies have had successes and others have had failures. Learning from these successes and failures is important in developing a successful and useful strategic personnel planning activity; experience which companies have had with strategic personnel planning provides precedents and guidelines for others.

The first guideline for effective strategic personnel planning is that personnel planning items must be based essentially on deductive analysis and they should be restricted to *observable trends* which, if continued, will inevitably lead to certain results. Thus, strategic personnel planning is based upon factual information and on the observation of trends which *now exist*, so that planning predictions *will* occur unless observed trends change.

Personnel planning, like all planning, must be monitored from time to time. If observed facts or existing trends change, then resulting forecasts must necessarily change also. Thus, strategic personnel planning is not a collection of guesses: it is based on fact, and what is observed must be monitored, with appropriate changes made when existing trends change.

Much of what will happen in the future which will affect the management of personnel will result from basic sociological, economic, and political trends. Facts and trends in these areas require large amounts of information and research conducted by professionals in various academic disciplines. Even large companies would not likely have the resources available or the resident know-how necessary to determine and monitor such information. Therefore, as a second basic guideline in strategic personnel planning, it is important to obtain basic sociological, economic, and political information and trends from those who conduct research and make reports in these areas. Such sources would include the United States Government, large financial institutions, and special research organizations, such as the Hudson Institute and the Rand Corporation. This is the beginning of the strategic personnel planning process.

As a third guideline, it is also prudent to obtain information from others, when possible and when it is already available, about general personnel planning data or trends. General personnel planning information has relevance for all firms and would have already utilized basic information on sociological, economic, and political trends and forecasts. If good work has already been done on personnel information which applies to all firms, there is no need to do the work again. In these matters, the "make or buy" decision clearly favors buying; provided, of course, quality information is available.

From general strategic personnel planning information, each firm's own personnel staff must then evaluate such information and determine which items are most relevant to their own company. In the process of doing this, other personnel planning items which are unique to their own firm might be identified. All planning items must then be translated into specifics for that firm.

Strategic personnel planning is an activity which demands very broad knowledge and experience in personnel. It is work which can only be done by senior personnel professionals. Furthermore, just as the chief executive officer is the only person who ultimately makes specific strategic planning decisions for the business overall, the senior personnel executive in a firm must be the one who manages the strategic personnel planning for his firm. This is the fourth guideline for effective strategic personnel planning of this type.

A fifth guideline is to use appropriate planning periods. There are actually three cycles that are relevant in strategic personnel planning. One covers a 20- to 30-year period. It is in this period of time when basic sociological, political, and economic trends evolve, and this period approximates a "generation gap." Planning for this cycle requires only identification of personnel planning items, general descriptions, and gross data estimates. Rarely would action steps be identified. This is the "early-warning" aspect of strategic personnel planning. Items which would likely impact the firm in 20 years or more only become personnel planning items to be tracked. They provide a factor to consider in making personnel decisions and may be the basis for not taking certain actions.

The second long-term personnel planning period is clearly more than five years; for most personnel planning items it would be a seven- to ten-year period. It is this time period which is practical for identifying and forecasting items which will impact the management of personnel and predict rather specifically how each item will impact the business. For these items, specific and detailed supporting data is usually required, the relevance to the firm described, a sketch made of actions required, and a schedule made for actions to be taken. Items likely to impact the firm in about seven to ten years need to be tracked carefully, and rather specific action plans should be formulated.

There is a third cycle of about three years. This cycle is typically the lead time required to implement actions to deal with emerging trends and to bring about significant changes in company programs and practices to deal with such items effectively. Because strategic personnel planning items don't occur at a point in time, but in a period of time, these items have really passed from the planning stage to the action stage.

As a sixth guideline, personnel planning must be an ongoing process. There is the initial start-up effort—the development of the original plan. This is a major effort. The initial project involves mostly the time costs of senior personnel people, which is an alternate use of time cost. It requires six months to a year of elapsed time to complete and may involve as much as $50,000 in expenses, services, and consulting fees.

Once the strategic personnel planning activity is on-stream, annual costs are moderate. This mostly requires monitoring trends and developments and periodic reviews of planning items. While personnel planning is an ongoing process, it does not require an equal increment of time and effort each year. It is an activity which can be cut back in some years and emphasized in others.

Finally, the organization for strategic personnel planning is important. As noted, the personnel director must be the "project leader" of strategic personnel planning and must make those decisions and conclusions as to what is relevant for the company and the actions to be considered. The personnel director would likely have a project team which would include key corporate personnel staff department heads, field personnel people, and others, as required, from such areas as finance and engineering. Included in the project team should be outside people when they have something specific to contribute. Like most project groups, each project member has his own mission, and the membership of the project group will change with time as the tasks change.

PERSONNEL PLANNING ITEMS SHOULD BE EVALUATED

The end product of personnel planning is the identification of trends which are occurring and future events which will result that are relevant to the management of personnel. Not all the resulting items are equal, either in their likelihood of occurring or in their relevance to the firm. Therefore, each item of personnel planning must be evaluated by four criteria:

1. Each planning item must be evaluated in terms of the prob- ability of the event occurring. Some personnel planning items are certain to occcur. If they have less than a fifty-fifty prob- ability, they probably should not be included in the person- nel plan, but rather they should be an item for future monitor- ing.

2. The reliability of the information upon which the planning item is based must also be evaluated. Different sources of information are not equally valid and reliable. Different items are based on data or information which inherently has differ- ing degrees of reliability and validity. Some items are subject to greater change. These factors must be identified and eval- uated in the strategic personnel plan.

3. The importance of each item to the particular company must also be evaluated. If a personnel planning item has no relevance for a firm, it shouldn't be included at all; unless it will have a broad impact on other firms or it will have a derivative impact on the future of that business. Others may be important but have minor impact on your firm. Some items may determine not only the success but also the survival of a business. These judgments are obviously important in translating personnel planning items into personnel planning activities.

4. Finally, the company must evaluate the cost and the effectiveness of possible company actions to deal with each planning item. There may be some items where the costs would be prohibitive or simply greater than the value of effective actions. It is also important to consider the impact of the actions. Might actions to deal with planning items cause changes or reactions which are themselves a problem?

Development of the strategic personnel plan requires the collection and analysis of a great deal of supporting data. The final product should not be a thick volume of data and descriptions which only the authors understand and which few have time to digest. Successful plans of all kinds, including successful strategic personnel plans, are simple and usually documents of a half-dozen pages, perhaps distilled from hundreds of pages. The final plan represents the *essential* items of great relevance and brief descriptions of actions to be taken.

ITEMS OF STRATEGIC PERSONNEL PLANNING

About four dozen strategic personnel planning items of possible relevance to firms in general have been identified. Company planning should consider all such items and identify those which are most relevant for their own firm by the evaluation process described. The potential importance of strategic personnel planning and the planning process itself can perhaps be best illustrated by identifying some of the planning items. A dozen items are summarized for illustrative purposes.

1. *People will earn a great deal more by the year 2005*: In the year 2005, the minimum wage will probably be $12.50 an hour. A secretary will earn $60,000 a year. MBA's without experience will start at $120,000 a year. However, it will likely cost $6 to ride a subway in New York City and local telephone calls may be $1.50. The very magnitude of these dollars has implications to the design and administration of compensation programs.

   The probability of these earnings levels is very high. The reliability of the data upon which they are based is also extremely good and can easily be monitored each year. The relevance of the information is intermediate, and the ability of most companies to deal effectively with this item is high.

2. *Taxes will be higher; much higher*: In the year 2005, college graduates without experience will start at a salary level where their incremental tax rate will be at the maximum; and the maximum will be more than 50 percent. All taxes paid, as a percentage of earnings will be 20 percent higher at the beginning of the 21st century than they are now.

3. *Employee productivity will increase*: The decline in employee productivity which started in the middle 1970s and which has continued into the 1980s will probably level out in the mid-80s and increase gradually from 1985 through 1990. After 1990 there will probably be a renewed growth in employee productivity.

   The upward trend in employee productivity will be due primarily to productivity improvement by the more effective treatment of personnel. Starting in the early 1990s, productivity will increase because of massive capital substitution in such areas as information processing, robotics, automated offices, and basic research breakthroughs, primarily in chemistry.

225

4. *There will likely be zero growth in real earnings**: A zero growth in real earnings will be an improvement over the decline in the real earnings of American workers in recent years. However, it will create great difficulties in the effective management of compensation; for instance, in managing pay plans designed to reward high-performers.

5. *Government health insurance will be enacted*: National health insurance will probably be a part of our economic life. Hopefully, it will be an insured system, soundly financed. It will likely only deal with the payment of health services, rather than the delivery of health services.

6. *The "cottage" work force will reemerge*: Approximately 5 percent of all those employed by corporations will not be on the company payroll. In some industries, this may be as high as 20 percent of the work force. A minority of such workers will work at home; it will be a rare event to hire a family work group. Rather, companies will contract out work; a major new "industry" will evolve.

7. *A "confrontation" between workers and nonworkers is likely*: The historic confrontation has been between workers and managers. In the future, the basic confrontation is likely to be between workers (including management workers) and nonworkers. This has profound implications on the nature of labor-management relations and the role of unions in our society.

8. *Large numbers of middle-level workers will become unemployable*: Sometime during the next 25-year period, there will be a large number of middle-level people who will become unemployed and who will be unemployable at anywhere near their former level of responsibility and pay. They will be obsoleted by information sciences. These people will have to be trained for new careers, at a considerable cost.

---

*Real earnings will be flat while productivity increases, due mainly to continued increases in transfer payments from workers to nonworkers.

9. *Facilities will be redesigned and relocated*: There will be important changes in the optimum size of facilities. The trend will be toward much smaller operations. Location of facilities will also change, resulting in locations that are more convenient for workers. This will reduce employees' transportation costs considerably and may contribute to worker immobility.

10. *Formal reeducation will be as common as skills training*: We will almost certainly see formal reeducation programs for professional people, both in recognized academic disciplines and in business disciplines. This will likely result in "universities" operated off-site by established educational institutions. It will end the era of professional obsolescence. This will result in a shift from a shortage to an oversupply of some engineering disciplines. It will also turn higher education into a growth industry.

11. *There will be more government regulation of business*: Comparable worth will be an issue of the past by the year 2005. There will likely be restrictions on hiring employed workers and on facility closings.

    Perhaps more significant than the items of greater governmental regulation will be the method. There will be few, if any, major new laws affecting employee relations. Instead, the greater amount of regulations of employee relations by the government will come from specific items attached as a rider to another bill and the increasing power of regulatory agencies. The courts will also have a major impact on the control of employee relations.

12. *Unfilled jobs*: At any point in time there are unfilled jobs, simply because there has not been time to fill the jobs: "frictional" shortages of workers. "Structural" shortages of workers have also emerged: jobs that cannot be filled. Structural shortages will be more than 5 percent of the work force.

This is just a sample of strategic personnel planning items; less than one-third of all I have been able to identify. Keep in mind that these are items *which will occur*; because current observable trends will make them inevitable.

Chapter 18

PERSONAL VALUES IN PERSONNEL WORK

In the personnel work we do in business, the focus is on personnel practices; what to do and how to do it. What we do is in response to a business need or problem, or because someone thinks there is a better way of doing something. Our motivation is what is good for the business. What's "right" is what improves business results.

PERSONAL VALUES AND PRODUCTIVITY

The "bottom line" must, in fact, always be dominant in our thinking and in our work. Management's goal in personnel relations must always focus on full or optimum utilization of the human resources of the enterprise: to see to it that employees work as effectively as possible. Management's goal must necessarily be the goal of those in personnel. But I question whether a firm will ever achieve that goal unless there are basic values underlying their employee-employer relationships. I think that the "effectiveness of work" goal is correct; but that there will be ineffectiveness in work unless there are also values in work experiences.

What I am suggesting is that in business we must consider personal values as well as the effectiveness of personnel practices in our work. I think that each is an essential input to what we do in personnel management, and each is necessary to achieve high levels of work effectiveness and productivity. Personal values and business needs do not have to be considered in equal portions. But personal values must be *a* consideration. At the present time such values are not considered sufficiently, are considered as a random factor, or are not considered at all.

What do "personal values" mean? Very broadly, they mean human values that value humans. They mean appropriate relationships between people; managers and workers, stockholders who own the wealth and employees who create the wealth. They mean consideration of the basic values of truthfulness, consideration, and concern as between all the stakeholders of the firm. Personal values are to the management of personnel in the contemporary businesses what our Bill of Rights is in politics, or what the Ten Commandments are in the Judeo-Christian religions.

There isn't any thought to urge the "humanism" which has pervaded the literature of business from time to time, and which occasionally finds itself into the practices of management. The concern of "personal values" is to do *right* rather than to be a *do-gooder*. Forget the view that managers should make people happy. Don't bother to look after others; but in work give them an equal opportunity to look after themselves. And dissuade yourself of the notion that somehow managers can make better people: this is business and not theology.

I think you can argue for "personal values" in business practices on two grounds. You can argue on the basis that it is the right thing to do. You can also argue on the ground that it is the effective thing to do. I prefer to focus on the latter, because it is more tangible and more provable.

THE NEED FOR PERSONAL VALUES

I think that inputting personal values into personnel practices is the effective thing to do. For a number of reasons, I think it is essential if, indeed, there is to be effective work. The reasons I would recommend that you must consider are:

1. Human assets react, and they tend to react in kind.

2. Those who work in your firm know things about their work

and themselves which are essential to optimizing results. Absence of personal values impedes or shuts off that critical and unique knowledge flow.

3. The absence of "personal values" inevitably results in an adversarial relationship which is the antithesis of effectiveness.

4. Application of personal values is a key to optimizing the traditional strengths of our society.

5. Ours is also largely a religious society. The conduct of corporate life must be consistent, or at least not inconsistent, with basic religious teachings.

These represent a pass-over identification of why a "personal value system" is an indispensable part of effective work. Each item needs more examination and a rigorous critique; and there need be some consideration of other possible reasons why we need personal values. The five items that have been identified will suffice for now and need only be summarized for illustration.

People are unique assets in a number of important respects. Perhaps most of all, however, people are the only assets of a firm which care how they are used and which react to how they are used.

Psychologists tell us that there is a human response to just about every stimulus; which, I am told, means that people react and that most of the time they react in kind. Believe this, because all psychologists tell us it is so; but believe it also because it is our experience. If you show little respect to someone, he can't have much respect for you. If you act superior to others, they will not likely think of themselves as inferior, and they will take every opportunity to prove it.

"Do unto others as you would have them do unto you" is really a nice way to live. It is also practical. If you don't do unto others as you would have them do unto you, then they will likely do unto you as you do unto them.

People have many choices at work in the way they react, and this is becoming more true as a larger portion of our work force consists of knowledge workers. Managers generally assume that if people don't like the way they are treated they will leave. Some do quit, but employees have other choices and may have good reasons to exercise one of those other choices. In many different ways at many different times, I have heard it said, "Our best people just don't leave." That isn't usually true, but it frequently isn't relevant because many employees have chosen another way to react. For example, they may stay with the firm but consciously do less than their best, or they may smile in your face but take advantage of opportunities to be subversive.

Top executives simply cannot comprehend the degree to which people throughout the organization deliberately do poorer work than they could or far less than their best as reactions to how they have been treated. We can't begin to estimate the cost to the firm of people doing less than their best. I think that much of this costly malaise of attitude has evolved over time because of the absence of personal values in the way business manages personnel.

Most managers know that those who work in the firm know things about their work and about themselves that no one else knows, or doesn't know as well, that are critical to optimum output. What many managers don't believe or frequently forget is that people won't necessarily volunteer what they know for the good of the operation, even if it may improve the operation very much. In the past ten years, many firms have increased productivity greatly through some method of worker involvement. They credit the technique or the method, and that is important. But I also think that the very effort injected some personal values, such as respect and trust, into the working relationship, and that this was critical in getting from workers what they knew all along.

Some of my colleagues in the field of personnel are proud of the productivity improvement programs and practices they have been a part of. I share their pride, but regret that such programs were necessary in the first place. So many of the work rules that resulted in poor productivity came into being because of promises that were made and broken, exploitation, favoritism, and disinterest in those who worked for the firm.

Forty years ago, there was a great deal of hate for the Japanese because we were at war with them and they were winning. Today, we have a love affair with the Japanese because we are locked in an economic struggle with them and they are winning again. But many of the things the Japanese do so well are tied to their own traditions and culture. It is an error to ape them when our traditions and culture are so different. We have some great strengths in our society that have contributed massively to our past successes, and it seems tragic to turn our backs on these strengths now when they are so badly needed.

We are not very far away from generations of farmers and frontiersmen, so we have a strong entrepreneurial desire. Ours is a free-choice society, and we are comfortable and competent at making decisions. Ours is a tradition of self-reliance and responsibility; and the strong work ethic was as much a part of our economic successes as our resources. We need to build work practices and personnel practices based on these characteristics of our society. But I think that we will never unleash these assets unless we build into our work systems another historic national characteristic—values.

In *Megatrends*, John Naisbitt talks about "high-tech, high-touch," which I would only change to "higher-touch." There has always been a need for high-touch; caring person-to-person relationships. We lost sight of that need sometime in the era of industrialization and then automation, and it cost us dearly. With high-tech workers, we cannot overlook the need for person-to-person relationships and, in fact, we need higher-touch.

We covet our freedom highly, to the point where we tend not to notice that we are losing it at a very rapid rate. We think of ourselves as individuals, to the point where we don't see, day by day, that our massive bureaucratic government and an increasingly rule-oriented society are creating a more and more dehumanizing experience and environment. Yet we still think of ourselves as free individuals and expect that everyone, including the "company," will recognize that. Values on the part of all people in the work situation (including management) are essential to a society of free individuals. The higher the position and the authority of the individual, the more important the values are; and it is critical that the leaders of business conduct themselves in a way that reflects high personal values. The higher level the person, the higher the standards; and that is *the* lesson of Watergate.

Finally, ours is a religious society. In fact, we are now going through a revival of religion. Whatever your religion, it is based on values. Religions have many things in common, and one of them is that they all teach that "good" is based on high "values." That is what we are taught to believe, and we believe that this is what we should experience in our work.

DO PERSONAL VALUES CONTRIBUTE TO HIGHER PRODUCTIVITY?

Recognize that effective work is a personal value in itself. Certainly, greater effectiveness of work will never diminish values. The two—values and effectiveness—are interrelated.

Those who work effectively and do their best have rewards. Good is so often its own reward. Those who do their best must have greater self-esteem than those who don't. Those who do their best have pride, regardless of other material rewards. And those who consistently do their best often surprise themselves with their achievements. Thus, effective work contributes to personal values.

The fact that values contribute to greater effectiveness of work is a more difficult case to prove. I have never been able to *prove* beyond a reasonable doubt to anyone that the injection of values into the business system and its personnel practices will demonstrably improve effectiveness of work. But I think that what can be proven, by logic and by experiences, is that the *absence* of values *diminishes* productivity. Therefore, concentrate on the question of whether high levels of productivity in a work environment can be sustained without personal values. If you look at cases as I have, then I think you will conclude as I have that the absence of personal values makes sustained high levels of productivity impossible and appears to result in work effectiveness that is unsatisfactory.

I would urge someone in the academic community to do research on the impact of personal values on productivity. We need to know more. All I know now is that personnel people

233

who work in operations—out in the "trenches"—tell me what I thought I knew when I did that work: more personal values would contribute to higher effectiveness of work.

I would suggest that any firm that is inclined to agree conceptually or morally to the proposition that personal values should be injected into personnel practices should look beyond the concepts and the general propositions and evaluate proposed specific action steps. Each action step should be evaluated by its impact on the effectiveness of work, recognizing that another purpose was to inject values into working relationships. Don't consider a project; build personal values into the "culture" of the business, one action at a time.

PERSONAL VALUES

It is necessary to identify what the values might be. Some seem so obvious. Others that may be just as important to effective work and to those who do the work are not obvious at all, and reasonable people may differ about what the values are and how important they are. Here are a few personal values which seem to me to be essential.

One value that seems obvious and essential is that the company and all of its spokespersons should always tell the *truth*. Actually, I have worked for hundreds of companies over the past thirty years and rarely have I seen companies that deliberately and consciously lied to their employees. But not lying is not enough. The firm and its officials must consistently be truthful.

For example, every personnel professional I know believes that effective employee communications are essential to productive work. But as we have already noted, for communications to be effective, they must be believable. Information communicated won't be believable unless the company tells the truth all the time.

Companies always tell the truth when it is favorable and makes the company and its management look good. In fact, companies tend to tell those truths over and over again. Business must also tell the truth to employees about things that are not favorable, or when they know employees will think differently, or even if they think the truth may cause trouble or dissatisfaction.

234

There is a very simple test for determining whether your firm tells the truth to its employees. Examine a sample of communications to employees. See if there are any instances when the company said, "I don't know," or "We made a mistake," or "We are telling you this because it is important, even though we know that many employees will not like what we say." Unless you find instances where the company has made all three of these statements, then one of two things is true: you have a perfect company or you have not told your employees the truth all of the time.

A second personal value is *respect*; respect for every single person who works in the firm. I think there must be respect in the usual sense of the acceptance of each person's own personal values, thinking, and beliefs. But in employee-employer relations there must also be a particular type of respect. There must be an inherent assumption in the way the firm is run that every employee will do his best, that he is trustworthy, and that he is responsible.

In most firms today there is inherent disrespect in some personnel practices. These were described in Chapter 4. What these differences say is that there are some people (e.g., the executives) who can be trusted to do their best and to do the right things and that there are others who cannot be so trusted. In fact, most executives I have known really believe that, unless they are regulated, most lower-paid people would do far less than their best and would take every advantage of the company; while they, the executives, are responsible. But I always keep asking, "At what level of the organization do people become irresponsible?"

I believe that people at every level and in every income bracket are equally trustworthy. Furthermore, I put my money where my trust is and for many years ran my own company on that assumption. To do otherwise is to show disrespect—manifestly. This creates a "them and us" atmosphere and, at least to some degree, an adversarial relationship. Such distinctions, I fear, are also largely self-fulfilling. If you tell people often enough by your practices that they cannot be trusted, many will become less than completely trustworthy.

There must be *equivalency* of treatment of every person in the firm. We know that some people in any business are more equal than others; e.g., some get paid more than others. But all such distinctions must be based on economic needs or operational requirements.

We must truly adhere to a philosophy of nondiscrimination based on race, creed, color, sex, national origin, weight, appearance, or anything else. We must do this beyond the requirements of the law: these should also be the values of the firm. The only basis for discrimination should be qualifications and effectiveness; the only prejudice should be for achievers and those who already have made commitments and contributions to the firm.

We all have our prejudices, and to say otherwise is to say that we are not human and not willing to learn from experiences. Personally, I don't like homosexuals or extreme women's libbers. But in work, I must treat them equally with machos and male chauvinists; and, in fact, I did when I owned my own company.

There must be a *commitment* by the company to every employee. It must be clear and visible. We know that to get optimum productivity requires a commitment to excellence by everyone who works in the firm. Very often, the needs of the organization require a level of commitment by people that has a cost to their personal lives, but it must be. Employees may be asked to do work they do not choose to do, or to go somewhere they would rather not go, for the good of the company and to help create shareholder values; sometimes at the cost of their own values.

We ask for a commitment from those who work in the firm and know we must have it to achieve the goals of the firm. Doesn't it follow, therefore, that to get this level of commitment requires a commitment in kind from the company? I think so, which is why I think some type of commitment by the company to its employees is another essential personal value.

When a firm brings an employee into the company, for example, I think it has an obligation to help that person be successful. Usually that serves the business interests directly, but I think there should be such a commitment even when there is a cost to the company. Another example: no company can guarantee jobs unless its customers guarantee sales. But a company can make a commitment to preserve jobs through economic adversity far greater than most are willing to do. This may mean, for example, shared work, which management finds inconvenient. Preserving more jobs in bad years may mean lower earnings per share than might have been possible for one quarter or one year.

There must also be a very special form of *concern* on the part of the company for those who work in the firm. The company must recognize every employee as a person, and that very much of the total person is a function of what happens away from work. Of course, the company must always expect the best work possible from every employee *under the circumstances*; but the recognition I urge you to consider would be to view each of those employees as a person whose circumstances vary a great deal.

When our older son was killed by the actions of another in a tragic accident, we were astounded at the number of business associates who had had a similar experience. The death of a child affects you massively, and it certainly also affects how you do your work, for a longer period of time than I would have believed. I had known many of these business associates for a very long time, but, of course, I didn't know them at all. I had worked with some of them during the period of their tragedy, but never once did I consider that what appeared to be less than their best was more than they were capable of, under the circumstances.

Never should a company interfere with or judge an employee's personal life. On the other hand, we simply must recognize that each person has more than a work life. We must express pleasure for their personal successes; and give understanding and perhaps some compassion when they experience tragedy or difficulty.

Since we have lived in Vero Beach, many clients have come here for consulting sessions and more have come to Florida for our conferences. This has given us an opportunity to get to know them as people as well as colleagues, and they us. We have found in every case that the whole person is better than only that part you see at work. It is a better and warmer way to work and live. Of course, that reduces in no way the obligation to do effective work. To the contrary, we have found even a greater responsibility to those we know than to those who just pay us.

A business is an institution that necessarily has its policies (i.e., the business version of laws) and its rules. I find that most firms have too few policies that mean anything in personnel management and far too many rules. But a firm must have both and, in combination, have a lot of them. I think it is critical, as a personal value, that all rules have a *reason* and that they be applied with *justice*.

There cannot be justice and reason unless circumstances and conditions, as well as the rules, are factored into decisions. The rules must be clearly for the common purpose of business success, rather than enforcing someone's code of conduct or personal vision of behavior. The rules can never be for the purpose of enforcing authority or exercising power.

Without this personal value, necessary administration becomes a distraction from work. If there is injustice or unreasonableness, there will be time-consuming confrontations. For those who have never managed in operations or practiced personnel at the first levels of work in an organization, this may all sound easy, but, in fact, it is the most difficult of all values to implement.

It is also suggested that one of the personal values is that the company *accepts* all those who work in the firm as working associates, legitimate stakeholders; and, in a sense, partners in work. We know that stockholders own the company. But it is the producers—those who do the work—who *are* the company. This notion is a basic value which must also be a part of personnel management if there is to be a sustained high level of effectiveness of work.

Employee-stakeholders should be recognized monetarily; by success-sharing compensation plans. Even more important, this personal value must be recognized in day-by-day management by the reactions of managers: sometimes just a word will do it. None of this however, can be play-acted; it must be the natural reaction of a personal value built into the practices of management, based in part on a belief of those who manage that all employees are truly working partners.

It doesn't seem terribly radical to me that those who determine the results, by the work they do, should be valued in every way possible for what they do. And there are many ways by which this is possible. Because it is neither difficult nor radical, it is surprising how little it is practiced. In fact, business in this country has reached the point where those who work in the firm are treated as hired hands—and I can almost hear many business executives I know saying or thinking, "That's what they are."

To this, I can only point out; "Mr. Executive, that's what you are too." We are all hired hands in the sense that we are legally employees of the company and paid by the company. Those who want to operate their firms truthfully should, therefore, include themselves in the same category.

There have been times when I have heard or observed things in consulting with companies that made me wish I had never heard the word "employee." Actually, the word itself is benign: according to the dictionary, an employee is " . . . a person who works for another for pay." We all do that. But in business, and particularly big corporations, the word has taken on another meaning with subservience and inferiority inferred. This is why, in my opinion, regarding all employees as partners is another essential personal value.

Another of these personal values which is of great importance in my mind is that the firm must provide *opportunities* for those who work there. Opportunities must clearly be related to the needs and the realities of the business. They can't be manufactured. Therefore, they are always limited; and, in my experience, the opportunities of the firm—even rapidly growing, successful firms—are more limited than are the potential for personal growth and greater contribution of those who work in the firm.

While opportunities are necessarily limited by the firm, they must be fashioned and directed to the interests and ambitions, as well as the capabilities, of those who work there. And, in my opinion, the people themselves must be prime determinants of their ambitions. The firm operates as a facilitator; having an obligation to let all workers know what the real opportunities are and a responsibility to make decisions involving opportunities for employees in an impartial manner.

Finally, the firm must conduct its affairs in every way so that every employee can have *pride* in their firm. For example, you really can't expect those who do the work to build quality into a product that was designed to be of poor quality in the first place. You can't realistically expect employees to obey your rules if you, as a company, don't obey the law. And if you obey the letter of the law but not the spirit of the law, then don't be surprised if employees treat your rules similarly.

Those may seem like a lot of personal values to consider.

And you may think that I sound like a preacher. If so, you are entitled to ask, "Who does he think he is—Julius Rice?"

No sermon intended, but if there is a need for values, then the values themselves must be identified. They must be described enough so that we are all considering the same possibilities. Most of all, perhaps, they are the basis for considering specific action steps to build personal values into personnel practices.

What is suggested is that every firm consider personal values as one factor when developing or reviewing any personnel practice. Building personal values into personnel practices should not be a special project. It should be a conscious part of the culture of the firm.

Many specific practices have been identified in this book, particularly in Chapter 4. Each was presented as a practical business action to improve the management of personnel and increase the effectiveness of work; and probably when you read them you evaluated them in terms of their practical business worth rather than personal values. If so, then your very experience reinforces my belief that building personal values into personnel practices is not only the right thing to do but it is also the sound way to manage personnel.

ABOUT THE AUTHOR

Robert E. Sibson has been a consultant in the field of personnel for over twenty-four years. During that time he has worked personally for over 500 firms and has been responsible for thousands of projects in all areas of personnel. During his consulting career, Mr. Sibson has developed many important innovations and new plans in the field of personnel management.

Mr. Sibson founded Sibson & Company, Inc., in early 1960. Under his leadership, the firm grew to become one of the premier consulting firms in the country in the area of personnel. After almost twenty years as head of the firm he founded, Mr. Sibson passed on the ownership of Sibson & Company to his associates and is no longer connected with the firm in any way.

Since January 1979, Mr. Sibson has focused his efforts on "developmental projects"; practical research for more effective personnel management practices in key areas, such as productivity improvement, management development, and succession; organizational redesign; personnel planning; and management pay programs. Mr. Sibson also continues to perform client work in the field of personnel, using the client company's own staff as his project group.

He also holds three-day workshop conferences on personnel management and compensation in Florida; problem-solving workshop sessions; and field presentations. These are all highly cost-effective methods of doing some types of consulting work.

Much of Mr. Sibson's efforts are devoted to *The Sibson Report*, an information service covering personnel management and designed specifically for high-level personnel people and general management executives. This information service, sold on a subscription basis only, includes two regularly scheduled reports, briefs, special reports on timely issues, and a telephone/letter information service.

Prior to 1960, Mr. Sibson worked as a Division Personnel Manager for Raytheon Company, as Personnel Director for Schick Incorporated, as Assistant Director of Industrial Relations for Otis Elevator Company, and as a Consulting Associate for Simpson & Curtin.

Mr. Sibson received a B.A. degree from Yale University and an M.B.A. from the Wharton Graduate School of the University of Pennsylvania. He has written seven books and dozens of articles on the personnel field. He is a frequent speaker at management, civic, and personnel meetings.